Current
CONTROVERSII

The Internet of Things

Other Books in the Current Controversies Series

Agriculture
Attacks on Science
Domestic vs. Offshore Manufacturing
Fossil Fuel Industries and the Green Economy
The Gig Economy
Hate Groups
Holocaust Deniers and Conspiracy Theorists
Immigration, Asylum, and Sanctuary Cities
Libertarians, Socialists, and Other Third Parties
Nativism, Nationalism, and Patriotism
Sustainable Consumption

The Internet of Things

Andrew Karpan, Book Editor

GREENHAVEN PUBLISHING

Published in 2022 by Greenhaven Publishing, LLC
29 East 21st Street, New York, NY 10010

Library of Congress Cataloging-in-Publication Data

Names: Karpan, Andrew, editor.
Title: The internet of things / Andrew Karpan, book editor.
Other titles: Internet of things (Greenhaven Publishing)
Description: First edition. | New York : Greenhaven Publishing, 2022. |
Series: Current controversies | Includes bibliographical references and index. | Audience:
Ages 15+ | Audience: Grades 10–12 | Summary: "Anthology of diverse perspectives exploring
the potential uses and dangers of the Internet of Things."— Provided by publisher.
Identifiers: LCCN 2020050951 | ISBN 9781534507746 (library binding) |
 ISBN 9781534507722 (paperback) | ISBN 9781534507753 (ebook)
Subjects: LCSH: Internet of things—Miscellanea—Juvenile literature. |
 Privacy, Right of—Miscellanea—Juvenile literature.
Classification: LCC TK5105.8857 .I564 2022 | DDC 004.67/8—dc23
LC record available at https://lccn.loc.gov/2020050951

Manufactured in the United States of America

Website: http://greenhavenpublishing.com

Foreword   **11**

Introduction   **14**

Chapter 1: Is the Internet of Things Beneficial for Its Users?

Overview: What Is the Internet of Things?   **19**

Nicole Kobie

Examples of how the internet of things has entered everyday life in the modern world are endless. More and more moments of our lives are being turned into data, and all of that data is being collected somewhere. Everything is a computer, and our lives are more efficient than ever. But at what cost?

Yes: The Internet of Things Means We Can Do More

The Internet of Things Helps People with Disabilities   **23**

David Beren

Technology that uses the internet of things is currently at the forefront of finding ways to improve the lives of people with disabilities. It is opening up online worlds for the blind and making homes safer than ever for the physically impaired.

How the Internet of Things Upgrades the Transportation Sector   **26**

Brian McGlynn

Another way to immediately see the positive impact of the internet of things is to look at a business sector that's already been transformed by it: the transportation sector. The doctrine that superior data drives better transit outcomes is by no means contentious among those who move things. The more data they have to work with, the better.

The Internet of Things Lives Up to the Hype   **30**

Tim Wright

Technologies that use the internet of things have already become second nature for many, and most consumers have quickly moved past questions of when and how they would be adapted into products used in daily life. Cities are now being built "from the internet up" and are powered by massive fiber-optic networks.

No: The Internet of Things Is Too Disruptive

The Democratic Process Is Too Vulnerable for the Internet of Things   **33**

Laura DeNardis

In pre–internet of things technology, everything had a paper trail. Voting was never perfect, but every vote could still be recounted and, eventually, something close to the truth could come out. But if a digital election is disrupted, the truth may be impossible to find. The internet of thing may mean that everything is transformed into data, but when data is deleted, it can become hard to find.

Unplugging from the Internet of Things   **36**

Christianna Silva

Human and machine connectivity will soon become ubiquitous and unavoidably present in most people's lives, and it will become impossible for people to opt out. In addition to the security risks that entails, a world wired into the internet of things is a world that's less free.

Data-Driven Technologies Are a Solution in Search of a Problem   **39**

Andrea Castillo

Wearable technology and networked clothing sounds exciting and may prove to be helpful. But was anyone looking for smart jeans? At what point does technology cease to enhance our lives and instead serve as a way to be controlled by technology designers?

Chapter 2: Is Increased IoT-Powered Automation a Good Thing?

Overview: How IoT Will Transform How Industries Function   **44**

Calum McClelland

The industrial internet of things (IIOT) has massive potential to impact the global economy. It is believed that the IIOT will transform industries including manufacturing, oil and gas, agriculture, mining, transportation, and health care, which collectively account for nearly two-thirds of the world economy.

Yes: IoT Tech Makes Life Better

IoT-Powered Automation Will Change Commerce   **49**

Kayla Matthews

The widespread application of the internet of things will radically change the commercial world. Buildings in major cities will use automation to function more efficiently. Retail businesses will use location-based technologies to deliver geofenced recommendations and discounts to customers.

The Internet of Things Plugs In Communities of Color   **53**

Nicol Turner Lee

Some of the possibilities suggested by IoT-based technology offer the promise of eliminating disadvantages that result from the digital divide, which often disproportionly affect people of color. Twenty-four million Americans lack access to fixed, residential high-speed broadband services today, and the internet of things could be a big part of ending that.

No: IoT Threatens Financial Security

The Internet of Things Changes Whom Workplaces
Work For   **61**

Kayla Matthews

While IoT-powered technologies are likely to bring in as many jobs as they eliminate, the jobs they bring will require greater specialization and will often require workers to change their careers. And some workers may feel stripped of their free will, too, as technology powered by the internet of things often enables new varieties of technological surveillance that could be handily used by bosses and managers.

The Internet of Things Has Created an Ad World   **64**

Joshua A. T. Fairfield

The internet of things is all about collecting data, but that data rarely belongs to the people who create or use it. Reports have shown that the data that IoT-powered devices collect are often marketed to other companies that are trying to sell their own products. Like almost nothing else before it, IoT-powered devices threaten commonly held ideas of property ownership.

Regulatory Constraints on Fiber Will Inhibit the
Development of Smart Cities   **68**

Lauren McCarthy

Limitations on the ability of municipal governments to invest in innovative technology, especially an inclusive, ubiquitous fiber-enabled network, will pose problems for future smart cities. Artificial restrictions on public sector involvement in fiber prevent new models from even being tested, keeping consumers in the dark.

Chapter 3: Is the Internet of Things Sustainable?

Overview: How IoT Technologies Are Used to Combat Environmental Degradation   **76**

Sarath Muraleedharan

Environmental degradation is one of the biggest issues of our time, and it is fitting that IoT-powered technologies can offer solutions to that problem that have never before been thought possible. Wastewater can be monitored and managed. The soil content of farms can be continuously tracked.

Yes: IoT Technology Is Essential to Build a Sustainable Future

How IoT Technologies Can Make Cities Sustainable   **80**

Shufan Zhang

Sustainability for city planning is an idea that goes beyond the handling of natural resources and is about thinking of entirely new ways for cities for work. The internet of things will power the smart cities of the future. The data collected by IoT sensor networks will evaluate existing environmental conditions and will optimize environmental measurements.

How IoT Will Revolutionize Waste Management   **86**

Neil Sequeira

IoT-powered technology will be an essential part of making a city's everyday waste management operations more sustainable. Technical innovations promise to give insights to sanitation workers as sensor-enabled and internet-connected garbage bins will collect information on fill levels, temperatures, and locations.

"Smart Farming" Will Sustainably Feed the World   **90**

Savaram Ravindra

The internet of things is also poised to transform agriculture through the advent of "smart farming," a capital-intensive system of growing food cleanly and sustainably for the masses. With the help of IoT-based smart farming, crops can be monitored with the help of sensors and irrigated using automated systems.

The Internet of Food Will Change How We Eat   **95**

Nicholas M. Holden, Eoin P. White, Matthew C. Lange, and Thomas L. Oldfield

A fully-enabled internet of food will monitor conditions and analyze data to derive knowledge and will enable larger changes in how we think about food systems.

No: IoT Technology Is No More Sustainable Than What It Replaces

The Environmental Impact of the Internet of Things   **104**

Laura-Diana Radu

The internet of things is, first and foremost, an information and communication technology, also known as an ICT. ICTs have a fundamentally negative environment impact: they consume energy and they degrade the environment around them.

The IoT Means Too Many Servers   **117**

John Harris

By 2030, one projection estimates that operating digital services will outstrip the generation capacities of entire countries. The rise of IoT-powered technology only means that more and more parts of modern life will need more energy to run.

Chapter 4: Is Data Safe Inside the Internet of Things?

Overview: The Value of Data in the IoT   **122**

Patrick McFadin

In IoT-powered smart devices and sensors, every event can and will create data that is sent, consumed, and used by those devices. The real value of those devices is derived from the order in which those data points are created.

Yes: Data Can Be Kept Secure in the Internet of Things

Blockchain Will Make the IoT Secure   **128**

Nir Kshetri

While insecure IoT devices have already contributed to major cyber-disasters, the potential widespread adoption of blockchain systems in the tech device marketplace offers the promise of near impenetrable security.

If Challenges Are Addressed, the IoT Can Reach Its Full
Potential   **132**

Sachin Kumar, Prayag Tiwari, and Mikhail Zymbler

Many research studies have been conducted to enhance technology
through IoT. However, there are still a lot of challenges and issues that
need to be addressed to achieve the full potential of IoT.

Blockchain Technology Requires Permissionless Innovation
to Flourish   **144**

Nur Baysal

In order for the IoT to succeed, consumers must have confidence
in its security. We must cultivate an environment of permissionless
innovation. Support for disruption and technological change, rather
than a precautionary regulatory approach, will lead to innovation.

No: Data Isn't Safe in the Internet of Things

The Internet of Things Is Only as Secure as the Internet Is **149**

Temitope Oluwafemi

There remains no general consensus on how to implement security
on IoT-powered devices. As long as the web is still not secure, it's
impossible to expect the IoT to be secure either.

IoT Toys Are Endangering Children   **153**

Marie-Helen Maras

Increasingly sophisticated toys that rely on connection to the
internet of things put the privacy and security of children at risk.
Unsecured devices can allow strangers to talk to children, track their
movements, and share information to third parties.

There Are Interconnected Vulnerabilities of the Internet of
Things   **157**

UpGuard

Just as interconnectivity increases functionality by linking a series
of devices, that same interconnectivity also connects threats from
around the world in just the same way.

Organizations to Contact   **164**
Bibliography   **170**
Index   **173**

Foreword

"Controversy" is a word that has an undeniably unpleasant connotation. It carries a definite negative charge. Controversy can spoil family gatherings, spread a chill around classroom and campus discussion, inflame public discourse, open raw civic wounds, and lead to the ouster of public officials. We often feel that controversy is almost akin to bad manners, a rude and shocking eruption of that which must not be spoken or thought of in polite, tightly guarded society. To avoid controversy, to quell controversy, is often seen as a public good, a victory for etiquette, perhaps even a moral or ethical imperative.

Yet the studious, deliberate avoidance of controversy is also a whitewashing, a denial, a death threat to democracy. It is a false sterilizing and sanitizing and superficial ordering of the messy, ragged, chaotic, at times ugly processes by which a healthy democracy identifies and confronts challenges, engages in passionate debate about appropriate approaches and solutions, and arrives at something like a consensus and a broadly accepted and supported way forward. Controversy is the megaphone, the speaker's corner, the public square through which the citizenry finds and uses its voice. Controversy is the life's blood of our democracy and absolutely essential to the vibrant health of our society.

Our present age is certainly no stranger to controversy. We are consumed by fierce debates about technology, privacy, political correctness, poverty, violence, crime and policing, guns, immigration, civil and human rights, terrorism, militarism, environmental protection, and gender and racial equality. Loudly competing voices are raised every day, shouting opposing opinions, putting forth competing agendas, and summoning starkly different visions of a utopian or dystopian future. Often these voices attempt to shout the others down; there is precious little listening and considering among the cacophonous din. Yet listening and considering, too, are essential to the health of a democracy. If controversy is democracy's lusty lifeblood, respectful listening and careful thought are its higher faculties, its brain, its conscience.

Current Controversies does not shy away from or attempt to hush the loudly competing voices. It seeks to provide readers with as wide and representative as possible a range of articulate voices on any given controversy of the day, separates each one out to allow it to be heard clearly and fairly, and encourages careful listening to each of these well-crafted, thoughtfully expressed opinions, supplied by some of today's leading academics, thinkers, analysts, politicians, policy makers, economists, activists, change agents, and advocates. Only after listening to a wide range of opinions on an issue, evaluating the strengths and weaknesses of each argument, assessing how well the facts and available evidence mesh with the stated opinions and conclusions, and thoughtfully and critically examining one's own beliefs and conscience can the reader begin to arrive at his or her own conclusions and articulate his or her own stance on the spotlighted controversy.

This process is facilitated and supported in each Current Controversies volume by an introduction and chapter overviews that provide readers with the essential context they need to begin engaging with the spotlighted controversies, with the debates surrounding them, and with their own perhaps shifting or nascent opinions on them. Chapters are organized around several key questions that are answered with diverse opinions representing all points on the political spectrum. In its content, organization, and methodology, readers are encouraged to determine the authors' point of view and purpose, interrogate and analyze the various arguments and their rhetoric and structure, evaluate the arguments' strengths and weaknesses, test their claims against available facts and evidence, judge the validity of the reasoning, and bring into clearer, sharper focus the reader's own beliefs and conclusions and how they may differ from or align with those in the collection or those of classmates.

Research has shown that reading comprehension skills improve dramatically when students are provided with compelling, intriguing, and relevant "discussable" texts. The subject matter of these collections could not be more compelling, intriguing, or urgently relevant to today's students and the world they are poised to inherit. The anthologized articles also provide the basis for stimulating, lively, and passionate classroom debates. Students who are compelled to anticipate objections to their own argument and identify the flaws in those of an opponent read more carefully, think more critically, and steep themselves in relevant context, facts, and information more thoroughly. In short, using discussable text of the kind provided by every single volume in the Current Controversies series encourages close reading, facilitates reading comprehension, fosters research, strengthens critical thinking, and greatly enlivens and energizes classroom discussion and participation. The entire learning process is deepened, extended, and strengthened.

If we are to foster a knowledgeable, responsible, active, and engaged citizenry, we must provide readers with the intellectual, interpretive, and critical-thinking tools and experience necessary to make sense of the world around them and of the all-important debates and arguments that inform it. We must encourage them not to run away from or attempt to quell controversy but to embrace it in a responsible, conscientious, and thoughtful way, to sharpen and strengthen their own informed opinions by listening to and critically analyzing those of others. This series encourages respectful engagement with and analysis of current controversies and competing opinions and fosters a resulting increase in the strength and rigor of one's own opinions and stances. As such, it helps readers assume their rightful place in the public square and provides them with the skills necessary to uphold their awesome responsibility—guaranteeing the continued and future health of a vital, vibrant, and free democracy.

Introduction

> *"One day, the internet of things will become the internet of everything. The objects in our world might sense and react to us individually all the time, so that a smart thermostat automatically adjusts based on your body temperature or the house automatically locks itself when you get into bed. Your clothes might come with connected sensors, too, so that the things around you can respond to your movements in real time."*
>
> —*Arielle Pardes*, Wired,
> *September 11, 2020*

Sometime in 2016, start-ups started selling smart collars for dogs. These kinds of collars were marketed as an upgrade to their colorful, analog predecessors and came equipped with a system of GPS trackers, heat sensors, and accelerometers that promised to tell their owners exactly how their pets felt at any given time.

This was not an incredibly new sort of technology: location tracking has been possible since the 1980s, and the technological insights provided were no more sophisticated than those that could be provided by a capable veterinarian. What was new was the ability to connect these tools together in a single strip of affordable, wearable plastic, relaying information to users who downloaded a cell phone app. Now that man's best friend could communicate data directly into the palm of their owners, one journalist suggested that the dogs of the future would be not unlike Tamagotchis—a pearl-colored miniature toy gadget popular in the 1990s—that could ape the needs of household pets.[1]

As of this writing, smart collars have yet to take the gadget or pet care market by storm. But this invention remains one of the many possibilities made purchasable by the internet of things. As an idea, it can feel hopelessly silly. Most pet owners, for instance, are probably attached to the idea of tending to their pets themselves for the same reason they got them in the first place. However, it is useful to think of the internet of things in just those terms: an argument that insists that things could be better computerized.

What would such a world look like? As the tech writer Bruce Schneier observes in his book on the subject, it is becoming less and less possible to buy a new car that is not, in fact, a computer with car programming attached.[2] The difference can seem almost unobservable, but it exists nonetheless in the small details. A car's major functions—the ignition, the brake pedal, the steering wheel—were once physical parts of a complex mechanical system that moved it one way or another. In most new cars, they are now a collection of buttons and sensors that are not unlike the lock button on a cell phone or the keys on a computer's keyboard. This is the world of the internet of things, simmering under the surface of today's technology. Cars can no longer be stolen by local thieves handy with a pair of spark plug wires but can be hacked by anyone in the world with the sufficient technical knowledge.

For Schneier, the "internet of things" is a clumsy phrase. He replaces it with a more tech-savvy title: the internet+ (internet plus).[3] This is a helpful way of thinking about the internet of things, nonetheless, as an extension of what technology has already made possible but can now be applied to more and more facets of life. The same technological thrust that brought the internet to the majority of the world's population can be used to bring it to even more people. Homes can be automated the way offices and stores have long been. Farms and mom-and-pop businesses can be run with the same clear-eyed efficiency as a microchip factory. Elections can be tallied with the digital certainty of a credit card transaction.

Of course, any user knows that credit cards are hardly secure. Rare is the customer who has not had their credit card number stolen and misused, and these are the concerns that now pervade the internet of things. Anything that deals in data can now be stolen. Yet most of us have decided there are fewer risks in carrying a credit card than in carrying a few hundred dollars in cash around with us. That said, a stolen credit card number can levy far more damage than a pickpocketer. The credit limit can be maxed out and, if unpaid, one's ability to spend money can be permanently diminished. To assuage fears that could keep us from shopping, Congress passed the Fair Credit Billing Act in 1974, and most credit card companies now strive to make their systems for reporting illegitimate use as customer friendly as they can. In a way, this is a kind of quiet insurance system that underlines a system of insecurity—paid for by merchants who are either presumably rewarded with increased sales or simply, at this point, do not have a choice.

But elections in a democratic society are not insured. Consequently, the move to conduct elections digitally is rife with fears over hacked ballots. Unlike ballots that are printed, digital votes cannot be recounted. It is worth remembering that, in the past, most fraudulent ballot boxes were merely *stuffed*. In the most well-known voting error in American political history, during the 2000 presidential election, irregularities in a small number of punch-card ballots just so happened to shift enough votes to change the result of incredibly narrow election. And allegations about fraudulent voting and a "stolen election" in 2020, though completely unproven even after extensive recounts, sparked an insurrection at the US Capitol by outgoing president Donald Trump's supporters. Given the political climate, would Americans ever embrace digital voting?

Arguments that suggest the internet of things be approached with caution instead of enthusiasm, some of which are collected in this resource, consequently argue that merely doing things more efficiently will not change the underlying threats of bad actors and bad decision making. Instead, they will only exacerbate them. A hanging chad can alter a few thousand votes, but a technological glitch could irreversibly alter millions of votes, perhaps, without most of us ever knowing.

The viewpoints presented in *Current Controversies: The Internet of Things* suggest that the internet of things is neither wishful thinking nor an imagined cure for society's ills. Instead, it is the world as it exists right now. And with these new computers come new debates, new questions, and new answers.

Endnotes

1. Anthony Cuthbertson. "This Smart Collar Turns Your Pet into a Living Tamagotchi." *Newsweek*, 4/12/16. https://www.newsweek.com/smart-collar-pet-kyon-tamagotchi-gps-dog-446754

2. Bruce Schneier. *Click Here to Kill Everybody*. New York, NY: W. W. Norton, 2018.

3. Ibid, pp. 8–9.

CHAPTER 1

Is the Internet of Things Beneficial for Its Users?

Overview: What Is the Internet of Things?

Nicole Kobie

Nicole Kobie is a freelance writer based in the United Kingdom whose work has appeared in the Guardian *and* Wired UK.

A mong its many other cultural and economic assets, Google is accumulating a rather comprehensive record of what is troubling us, from asking the search engine to diagnose our disease symptoms to whether we will ever find true love. It seems only natural, then, to turn to Google to decrypt the latest piece of technical jargon, "the internet of things."

It is a term that internet users have been peppering the search engine with questions about. But what does it mean for real life? We've taken the most commonly asked questions about the internet of things, and answered them using a real human being.

What Is the Internet of Things (And Why Does It Matter)?

The internet of things (or as it's also known, IoT) isn't new: tech companies and pundits have been discussing the idea for decades, and the first internet-connected toaster was unveiled at a conference in 1989.

At its core, IoT is simple: it's about connecting devices over the internet, letting them talk to us, applications, and each other. The popular, if silly, example is the smart fridge: what if your fridge could tell you it was out of milk, texting you if its internal cameras saw there was none left, or that the carton was past its use-by date?

Where it's most common, in Britain at least, is home heating and energy use—partially because the government is pushing energy companies to roll out smart meters (although it has been questioned whether it can be delivered on schedule). They have clever functions that let you turn on heating remotely, set it to turn down the temperature if it's a sunny day, or even turn off when there's no-one home. Some can tell the latter with motion-sensing cameras, or simply by seeing that your smartphone (and therefore you) has left the premises.

IoT is more than smart homes and connected appliances, however. It scales up to include smart cities—think of connected traffic signals that monitor utility use, or smart bins that signal when they need to be emptied—and industry, with connected sensors for everything from tracking parts to monitoring crops.

Why does it matter? There's a reason the government is encouraging energy companies to hand you a smart meter: all that data and automated use is more efficient, meaning we use less energy. Many areas of IoT show such benefits, though some smart gadgets are more about whizz-bang effects than efficiency, which may well be why we're seeing more smart heating than smart fridges in the UK.

Is It Safe? Can the Internet of Things Be Secured?

Everything new and shiny has downsides, and security and privacy are the biggest challenges for IoT. All these devices and systems collect a lot of personal data about people—that smart meter knows when you're home and what electronics you use when you're there—and it's shared with other devices and held in databases by companies.

Security experts argue that not enough is being done to build security and privacy into IoT at these early stages, and to prove their point have hacked a host of devices, from connected baby monitors to automated lighting and smart fridges, as well as city-wide systems such as traffic signals. Hackers haven't, for the most part, put much attention to IoT; there's likely not enough people using connected appliances for an attack against them to be worth the effort, but as ever, as soon as there's a financial benefit to hacking smart homes, there will be a cyber criminal working away at it.

So the short answer is yes, IoT is relatively safe: you're not likely to face serious loss or damage because of your smart meter, any more than your home PC, at least. However, there's no guarantee, and so far not enough is being done to ensure IoT isn't the next big hacking target.

How Will the Internet of Things Affect Business and Work?

This all depends on your industry: manufacturing is perhaps the furthest ahead in terms of IoT, as it's useful for organising tools, machines and people, and tracking where they are. Farmers have also been turning to connected sensors to monitor both crops and cattle, in the hopes of boosting production, efficiency and tracking the health of their herds.

The examples are endless, and all we can predict is that connected devices will likely creep into most businesses, just the way computers and the web have. When the efficiencies are with tools or plants, it's easy to appreciate the potential benefit, but when it's office workers who are being squeezed for more productivity, it could take on a bit of a dystopian shade: imagine your security access card being used to track where you are in the building, so your boss can tot up how much time you're spending in the kitchen making tea.

On the flip side, a smart tea maker that knows just when you're in need of a cuppa could be very handy indeed.

What Does the Internet of Things Mean for Healthcare?

Smart pills and connected monitoring patches are already available, highlighting the life-saving potential of IoT, and many people are already strapping smartwatches or fitness bands to their wrists to track their steps or heartbeat while on a run.

There's a host of clever connected health ideas: Intel made a smart band that tracks how much patients with Parkinson's shake, collecting more accurate data than with paper and pen;

Sonamba monitors daily activities of senior or ill people, to watch for dangerous anomalies; and people with heart disease can use AliveCore to detect abnormal heart rhythms.

Healthcare is one area where more data has the potential to save lives, by preventing disease, monitoring it and by analysing it to create new treatments. However, our health is also one of the most sensitive areas of our lives, so privacy and security will need a bit more preventative medicine first.

Is the Internet of Things Real?

This is perhaps the best query being Googled about IoT: is it real?

Surprisingly, it's tough to answer. Technology is full of marketing and hype—it's often difficult to decide early on whether an innovation is truly ground-breaking or not. After all, many tech pundits mocked the first iPhone.

But the internet of things is one of those wider ideas that isn't dependent on a single project or product. Smart fridges may well be the appliance of the future, or could fall by the wayside as too much tech for too little gain, but the idea of connected sensors and smart devices making decisions without our input will continue.

A decade from now, everything could be connected or perhaps only bits and pieces with specific benefits, such as smart meters; and we may call it IoT, smart devices or not call it anything at all, the way smartphones have simply become phones.

No matter where it is or what we call it, IoT is real—but what it will look like in the future is something even Google can't answer.

The Internet of Things Helps People with Disabilities

David Beren

David Beren is a freelance tech writer whose work has appeared on websites like Lifewire and IoT Tech Trends.

For years, the pace of rapidly advancing technology has often left behind individuals with disabilities. Fortunately, that seems to be changing with the rise of new technologies. There are new developments that will improve millions of lives. The advent of the Internet of things (IoT) is at the forefront of these advancements promising to improve accessibility for those who need it most. Let's take a look at just a few of the ways IoT advancements are leading to a promising future.

Reading Your Surroundings

Microsoft has always been at the forefront of technology, but the announcement of their "Seeing AI" is opening up a whole new world. For the visually impaired, this app will utilize the camera on an iPhone to describe objects in front of them. This incredible piece of IoT tech can announce a busy intersection, identify cash currency amounts, locate and scan product barcodes and recognize the emotions of people.

It's an incredible leap forward for the blind. Now they can interact with the world in a way that wasn't possible a few years ago. Converting the world to an audible experience is just one of the many ways IoT is improving the lives of the disabled.

"How IoT Can Help People with Disabilities," by David Beren, Uqnic Network, October 14, 2019. https://www.iottechtrends.com/how-iot-help-people-with-disabilities/. Reprinted by permission.

Access to Information

While many people might take products like Google Home or Amazon Alexa for granted, those with disabilities see them in an entirely different light. Connecting to the "cloud," these smart home products allow for near-infinite access to so many different types of information. Everything from search results, sports scores, movie times, playing music, making phone calls and so much more. Even more notable is the ability of these products to connect to other smart products around the home. Managing thermostats, speakers, and even garage doors through controls was once unheard of for those with disabilities.

Crossing the Street

While it may be a simple task for millions, crossing the street is often dangerous for those with disabilities. Fortunately, the rise of IoT technology is introducing new capabilities that are destined for global rollouts. The Netherlands is one such place where significant steps have been taken to protect those who need additional support.

Their "Crosswalk" system embeds sensors in traffic lights and connects to an app installed on a smartphone. Once enabled, this app recognizes when a disabled individual is approaching an intersection. It automatically adjusts the timing on the light signals to allow for more time to cross the road safely. Technologies like Crosswalk have enormous benefits for people who aren't often guaranteed extra help.

Smart Wearables

While the Apple Watch gets all the smart wearable glory, it's devices like the "Dot Watch" that are really taking a leap forward. Designed for those with both visual and audible challenges, this watch is bound to make life easier for millions. There are incredibly valuable features like telling the time and date, an alarm clock, or adding a timer and a stopwatch. Those might be apps we take for granted, but for people with disabilities, the opportunity to tell time on their wrist down to the second is a huge leap forward.

The same can be said for knowing who is calling instantly. As a call comes in, the watch vibrates and displays the name of the caller in braille. The same scenario plays out with text messages as they are translated to braille and forwarded on to the dot watch. Intuitive touch controls make it easy to read and scroll through a message. The best part of the dot watch is that it teaches braille on the go so it's inclusive for all.

Smart Environments

Products like the Philips HUE Light Bulb have exploded in popularity in recent years. It's no surprise the use of these lightbulbs has been overlooked for people with disabilities. However, for those with cognitive impairments, setting reminders with glowing lights can be game-changing. The lights can be programmed to glow blue when the doorbell rings or red for a fire alarm. Something so simple can improve lives for the disabled overnight. And it's still just one way that the world of IoT is leading toward a better future.

Conclusion

There's little question that the potential of IoT will help bridge the disability gap and lead to a more inclusive world. It's a foregone conclusion that we'll see IoT-enabled devices and technology continue to expand our world and improve our lives. The road remains long to equal the playing field for those with disabilities but with each leap in IoT technology, that gap closes bit by bit.

How the Internet of Things Upgrades the Transportation Sector

Brian McGlynn

Brian McGlynn is the chief operating officer of Irish software company Davra, which markets a platform for operating IoT-based infrastructure.

What can you say about the spread of the IoT in transportation? In short, this industry is pushing the limits that once defined it. Sure, most connected devices might not build new roads on their own or fuel the vehicles that traverse them, but the IoT does something equally advantageous. It improves the way companies, cities and nations maintain and utilize these assets so that the entire planet can benefit.

How can transportation sector organizations that adopt an IoT-centric business model ease common transit woes and deliver superior services? While it certainly helps to chart out a smart business plan, your use of distributed computing and data science could be the compass that enables you to make sense of the map. Here's how to go from simply watching the scenery whiz by to taking an active role in deciding what shows up outside your window.

Technology and the Transportation Sector

Most business technologies benefit from clear guidance and well-thought-out implementation strategies. Before you deploy a new vehicle fleet upgrade, for instance, you'll probably define an operating mission and identify which kinds of hardware will help you fulfill your objectives with the greatest ease.

In transportation, it's not always easy—or practical—to map everything out clearly in advance or separate individual aspects

"Internet of Things (IoT) in Transportation," by Brian McGlynn, Davra, November 13, 2019. Reprinted by permission.

of a greater business whole. For instance, the boundaries between marine shipping infrastructures and land-based transit systems aren't always as clearly defined as the ports that serve as their meeting points. Even within seemingly straightforward sectors, such as trucking and heavy rail, there exists a vast diaspora of management methodologies and business practices that dictate how freely different enterprises can leverage the tools they have at hand.

Can Better Data Steer You Past Technology Usage Challenges?

We're big fans of enabling those who prefer to do things their way. Still, this tendency to blaze your own path can definitely complicate technology adoption in freight, passenger transit, and other transportation domains. Even more troubling, today's enterprises are often driven by market factors that bear scant resemblance to ideal business conditions, such as when you're:

- Trying to accommodate population growth using an outmoded public transit system that was never intended to handle so many riders
- Working to identify failure-prone municipal assets before they succumb to wear and tear with disastrous consequences
- Deploying promising new transit technology that hasn't yet proven its safety or surmounted regulatory hurdles
- Attempting to secure and justify additional funding from stakeholders that don't understand the technical nuances that dominate your day-to-day operations

These sorts of challenges are prime candidates for IoT in transportation solutions, but finding answers takes more than just throwing advanced network hardware—or cash—at the problem. Legacy transportation control technologies, variable operating conditions and a host of location-specific nuances make it incredibly difficult to build comprehensive systems from the ground up. Enterprises and municipalities that want to steer clear of the road hazards on their path to a more efficient operation had better be prepared to overhaul their IT strategies.

Problem Solving with IoT in Transportation

Most transit industry optimization problems benefit from deep insights, and the doctrine that superior data drives better transit outcomes is by no means contentious. For example, the overwhelming majority of cities demand in-depth testing of autonomous vehicles before letting them travel their streets. Public transportation tracking helps improve service by decreasing wait times at subway platforms and bus terminals to increase ridership. Fleet managers track everything from fuel consumption to regularly planned maintenance calls to get the jump on machinery that will inevitably break down.

Good data has the power to keep companies rolling, sailing and flying more efficiently, and the quality of your information is wholly dependant on how finely tuned your data systems are. Let's look at a few quick examples that illustrate the benefits:

Delivering Happier Holidays

Shipping companies traditionally face extreme demand around the holiday season. Companies like FedEx and UPS have moved to satisfy their clientele by deploying GPS-enabled IoT applications. While delivery tracking has long been an industry standard, this switch enabled freight enterprises to improve their routing, stay better informed about cargoes en route and avoid traffic in realtime.

Riding the Rails More Safely

Railways changed the world by bringing access to remote locales, but many systems are the embodiment of brainless technology. A distant rail spur can't tell an engine operator when they're about to hit a washed-out section of track or fall afoul of a sleeper that's been rotting for decades. Finland's VR Group took a new approach. By adding sensors to everything from doors to axles and wheels, the state-owned rail operator was able to not only stay ahead of problems but also analyze their root causes to enhance savings and reliability.

Building More Rewarding Business Possibilities

Unique management problems plague trucking companies. More than any other industry, they're subject to the needs of distributed workforces that aren't always easy to manage, particularly when routes take drivers far from corporate headquarters.

Our team used Intel's OBD-II hardware to bring transportation businesses superior insights. By automating vital data-collection tasks, such as tracking driver mileage and behaviors, we devised solutions that helped fleet managers and policy providers make the most of usage-based insurance models. On top of enhancing safety, upholding smart user data ownership standards and easing the claims process, our pay-as-you-drive solutions help operators settle into comfortable, safe working routines.

Tips for a Better-Linked Tomorrow

According to our partner Intel, in 2020, the Internet of Things will include around 26 smart objects for every human on the planet. While only some of these devices will occupy the transit sector, the IoT in transportation is already empowering huge changes.

What are your odds of successfully leveraging linked computing to tie technology, business assets, and people closer together? Technological capability isn't an issue considering that modern sensors can accomplish everything from remotely monitoring the humidity and temperature inside cargo compartments to tracking individual palettes as they get offloaded and placed on specific vehicles. The ecosystem you build your IoT applications on top of is the only limiting factor.

The Internet of Things Lives Up to the Hype

Tim Wright

Tim Wright is director of technology at the Institute of Tele-communications Professionals, which calls itself the UK's leading independent institution for people who work in telecommunications.

For many of us, the internet of things (IoT) is becoming second nature, and even for those who have been waiting to see what happens, connected things are starting to impact our lives, regardless. The implementations of IoT are varied, from personal device connectivity through to connected homes, cars, factories and smart cities.

But just how far has this gone? Have the benefits lived up to the earlier hype, and what can we expect over the coming years? And what are the barriers to more widespread adoption?

The seminar held in the auditorium at BT Centre, London, was an opportunity to explore these questions and to get a greater insight into the reality of IoT. It was attended by about 90 people, with expert speakers from BT, Cisco and Connect Fibre.

Adam Thilthorpe, director of external affairs at the British Computer Society (BCS), spoke briefly about the partnering opportunities around the IoT.

He noted that the increasing reliance on IT and telecoms by individuals, companies and society as a whole places a huge responsibility on professionals in our industries to ensure that the developments are for the collective good.

BT chief researcher John Davies noted that with the costs of IoT sensors falling, power consumption decreasing, and the use of low-power radio access wide area network (LoRaWAN) technology to provide connectivity to sensors, we can expect to see a massive increase in the number of devices—as many have previously predicted.

"Implementing IoT—Overcoming Barriers to Commercial Adoption," by Tim Wright, TechTarget, July 4, 2019. Reprinted by permission.

The basic architecture of IoT comprises four domains: the sensors, the connectivity of those sensors, the data hub that enables the data from all sorts of sensors to be interoperable (rather than stuck in silos), and the applications.

The data hub plays a vital role in presenting the data to the applications in a uniform way, and Davies highlighted the work being done at CityVerve, a smart city demonstrator in Manchester encompassing a smart cycle light trial to understand cycle usage and improve cycle routes, an air quality trail which is linked to traffic density, and a water usage trial for leak management and demand management.

Edge computing will play an important role in reducing connectivity demands, and zero-touch device management will be essential.

Stuart Higgins, head of smart cities and IoT at Cisco, talked about some of the IoT trials and commercial deployments in the UK and worldwide. Many companies are digitising—seeing their operations and products as data to be managed in an IoT context. But only 40% of IoT projects make it past proof of concept for reasons of complexity, security or scale.

These are not insurmountable obstacles, but they do limit the initial application areas. For example, applications in local authorities are focused on air quality monitoring, bin collection, parking availability and street lighting.

Higgins noted that a proposed new town at Fawley, near Southampton, would be built "from the internet up," hopefully allowing greater opportunities for IoT deployment. Examples of commercial applications of IoT include intelligent transport systems, which can be used as showcases.

Full-fibre broadband expert and entrepreneur Stefan Stanislawski, managing director of recently established Connect Fibre, asked how a new fibre operator such as his could exploit or offer IoT capabilities.

Connect Fibre is an open access fibre operator that sells its capabilities to service providers, but for Stanislawski, sensor data connectivity is a low-value business opportunity. He usually applies a £100,000 rule to a business opportunity, and most telemetry projects fail to meet that threshold. One possibility might be to deploy LoRa on poles or cabinets as an add-on sales incentive. LoRa operates in the licence-exempt spectrum and has a considerable range.

I myself moderated the panel session, which explored a number of questions around the commercial case for IoT. Why do so few IoT projects make it past proof of concept? Is it that the ecosystem underpinning IoT is not sufficiently in place?

Local authority budget constraints in the UK have restricted smart city applications to smart lighting, parking and bins. The sensor connectivity solutions are reasonably well understood, especially with the use of LoRa. And the standards, particularly of the sensors, the data hub and application programming interfaces (APIs), are being actively addressed in ETSI and by the Network Vendors Interoperability Testing Forum (NVIOT).

Standardised interfaces and APIs are necessary to have the potential to separate the provision of sensors, connectivity, data hub and applications. However, security in such a multi-provider environment becomes the responsibility of all players.

All in all, the piece parts of the IoT ecosystem are falling into place and real-word commercial examples are now there to be seen.

The Democratic Process Is Too Vulnerable for the Internet of Things

Laura DeNardis

Laura DeNardis is the author of The Internet in Everything: Freedom and Security in a World with No Off Switch, *published by Yale University Press in 2020.*

The app failure that led to a chaotic 2020 Iowa caucus was a reminder of how vulnerable the democratic process is to technological problems—even without any malicious outside intervention. Far more sophisticated foreign hacking continues to try to disrupt democracy, as a rare joint federal agency warning advised prior to Super Tuesday. Russia's attempt to interfere in the 2016 election has already revealed how this could happen: social media disinformation, email hacking and probing of voter registration systems.

The threats to the 2020 election may be even more insidious. As I explain in my new book, *The Internet in Everything: Freedom and Security in a World with No Off Switch*, election interference may well come through the vast constellation of always-on, always-connected cameras, thermostats, alarm systems and other physical objects collectively known as the "internet of things."

The social and economic benefits of these devices are tremendous. But, in large part because the devices are not yet adequately secure, they also raise concerns for consumer safety, national security and privacy. And they create new vulnerabilities for democracy.

It is not necessary to hack into voting systems themselves but merely co-opt internet-connected objects to attack political

"'Internet of Things' Could Be an Unseen Threat to Elections," by Laura DeNardis, The Conversation Media Group Ltd, March 6, 2020. https://theconversation.com/internet-of -things-could-be-an-unseen-threat-to-elections-132142. Licensed under CC BY-ND 4.0.

information sites, stop people from voting, or exploit the intimate personal data these devices capture to manipulate voters.

Disrupting Political Communication

Connected objects have already been hijacked to shut down internet traffic.

The Mirai botnet of 2016 hijacked insecure video cameras and other home devices to launch a massive "distributed denial of service" attack that blocked access to many popular sites, including Reddit and Twitter. More recently, the FBI arrested a hacker for allegedly disrupting a California congressional candidate's website, flooding it with so many false requests it became inaccessible for legitimate views.

Similar political attacks that hijack some of the billions of often insecure connected devices could disrupt campaign websites and social media. They could also restrict public access to government websites with information about how and where to vote, as well as news reports on election results.

Preventing People from Voting

Beyond blocking access to political information, a foreign agent or group might seek to stop people from voting by creating targeted chaos, whether by disrupting power systems, generating false weather or traffic reports, or otherwise triggering local emergencies that divert attention on Election Day.

Smart cities and the industrial internet of things are already targets, as evidenced by the yearslong history of Russia-attributed disruptions to Ukrainian power systems. Hacking home alarm or water systems could create politically micro-targeted local emergencies that distract people who would otherwise vote.

This type of local disruption in swing districts would be more likely to evade public or press scrutiny than an outright hack of election machines or vote-tallying systems.

Making Phishing Hacks More Credible

The massive amount of intimate data these devices collect—when someone enters a building, drives a car, uses a sink, or turns on a coffee machine—could also make political operatives more susceptible to highly targeted spear phishing attacks. These tactics trick people into relinquishing personal information or clicking on malicious links—mistakes that gave hackers access to Democratic National Committee emails in 2016.

Similar phishing attempts on political campaigns continue, seeking to infiltrate email accounts used by presidential and down-ballot candidates. The more believable they are, the more effective they are—so an email referencing personal facts gleaned from connected objects would make these attacks more potent.

Not Being Surprised Again

More things than people are now connected to the internet. These connected objects are a new terrain for election interference—and people shouldn't be surprised if they're used that way.

To address this over the long term, customers will have to demand better privacy and security from their connected devices, such as doorbells and lightbulbs. Companies—and political institutions—that connect these devices to their networks will have to build in appropriate safeguards. Manufacturers will also have to design better protections into their devices. There may also need to be data privacy laws limiting how personal information is collected and shared.

More immediately, though, it is essential not only for state and local authorities and intelligence communities to remain vigilant, but for citizens to take security precautions with their own devices, and be on high alert for personalized attempts to influence or disrupt their political participation.

Preserving democracy now requires taking seriously the consequences of the internet being deeply embedded in the physical world—the internet in everything. We are all responsible.

Unplugging from the Internet of Things

Christianna Silva

Christianna Silva is a New York–based freelance writer and an associate editor on National Public Radio's digital news team.

After a long day, many of us try to set down our technology and unplug from the world around us. But, according to a new report by the Pew Research Center and Elon University's Imagining the Internet Center, over the next few years, that will become much more difficult to do.

Almost half of the world's population is connected online. And technology is constantly looming in our lives: the Nest thermostat regulates our household temperature, a camera watches our dogs, our health is constantly monitored, and technology keeps our houses safe when we're at work.

The Internet of things will continue to spread between now and 2026, until human and machine connectivity becomes ubiquitous and unavoidably present, according to experts who participated in what Pew described as a "nonscientific canvassing."

About 1,200 participants were asked: "As automobiles, medical devices, smart TVs, manufacturing equipment and other tools and infrastructure are networked, is it likely that attacks, hacks or ransomware concerns in the next decade will cause significant numbers of people to decide to disconnect, or will the trend toward greater connectivity of objects and people continue unabated?"

The answers they gave were telling: 15 percent said significant numbers of people would disconnect while 85 percent said most people would just move more deeply into connected life.

Survey Highlights

Unplugging Is Futile, and Plugging In Is Unavoidable
It's already difficult to create distance from the technology that surrounds us, but as connectivity increases, it might become impossible to do so.

Marti Hearst, a professor at the University of California, Berkeley, says just that.

"People's businesses, homes, cars and even their clothing will be monitoring their every move, and potentially even their thoughts," she says. "Connected cities will track where and when people walk, initially to light their way, but eventually to monitor what they do and say. The walls of businesses will have tiny sensors embedded in them, initially to monitor for toxins and earthquakes, and eventually to monitor for intruders and company secrets being shared. People currently strap monitors on their bodies to tell them how many steps they take. Eventually, all fluids in and out of bodies will be monitored and recorded. Opting out will be out of the ordinary and hugely inconvenient, just as not carrying a mobile device and not using a fast pass on the highway are today."

So once people are involved in the system, it's hard to get out of it. What if they didn't get involved at all?

Judith Donath of Harvard University's Berkman Klein Center for Internet & Society says that isn't actually a choice you get.

"People will move more deeply into connected life—and they also will be moved there whether they want to be or not," she says. "The connection of the physical world to information networks enables the collection of an unimaginably vast amount of data about each of us, making it possible to closely model how we think and to devise increasingly effective ways of influencing how we act and what we believe. Attaining this ability is extraordinarily valuable to anyone with something to sell or promote."

People Crave Connection and Convenience Over All Else, and Modern-Day Technology Serves This Well

People are used to risk, and most people believe bad things won't happen to them anyway.

David Clark, a senior research scientist at MIT and Internet Hall of Fame member, says: "Unless we have a disaster that triggers a major shift in usage, the convenience and benefits of connectivity will continue to attract users. Evidence suggests that people value convenience today over possible future negative outcomes."

What about technology hacks, like WannaCry and the Mirai bot?

Robert Atkinson, the president of the Information Technology and Innovation Foundation, says it probably won't bother users as much as you might expect.

"Most adults in the US drive cars even though it entails risks," he says. "Most adults will use IoT devices even though they involve risks because the benefits will vastly outweigh any potential risks. Moreover, as IoT progresses security will improve."

The Internet of Things Might Become Safer over Time

Many of the experts surveyed noticed that the Internet of things isn't particularly safe as-is, but will become safer as more people become aware of the issues.

Amy Webb, futurist and CEO at the Future Today Institute, writes: "Technology can be like junk food. We'll consume it, even when we know it's bad for us. There is no silver bullet. The only way to effectively prevent against malware and data breaches is to stay continually vigilant. To borrow an analogy from *Game of Thrones*, we need a 'Night's Watch' for security. Because when it comes to the Internet of Things and data breaches, 'winter is coming.' Organizations must hire enough knowledgeable staff to monitor and adjust systems, and to empower them to keep pace with hackers. IT and security staff must be willing to educate themselves, to admit when they need help and to demand that executives make decisions proactively."

Data-Driven Technologies Are a Solution in Search of a Problem

Andrea Castillo

Andrea Castillo is program manager of the Technology Policy Program for the Mercatus Center at George Mason University. She is a coauthor of Liberalism and Cronyism: Two Rival Political and Economic Systems *and* Bitcoin: A Primer for Policymakers.

Today's world of ubiquitous mobile applications, seamless multiplatform integration, and constant social feedback would be hard to imagine a decade ago, when your new cell phone's colored screen and grainy camera capabilities were sure to impress and perhaps begrudge your friends.

Remember that old Nokia 3310 and the hours of Snake you enjoyed? Compared to your latest glittering iPhone, it might as well now literally be used in building construction.

In ten more years, you'll probably feel the same way about your jeans.

Last week, Google revealed Project Jacquard, an exciting new initiative to literally weave the Internet into the very fabric of our clothes. Cutting-edge techies are teaming with the forward-looking fashion designers at Levi Strauss to lace tiny conductive fibers that can sense pressure and temperature, called Jacquard yarn, within our favorite denim garments and finally bring them into the 21st Century.

A small circuit board—no doubt discretely hidden in a button or garment lining by the clever threadsmiths at Levi Straus—will connect and process tactile inputs from the Jacquard yarn woven throughout the garment. Voilá! Your jeans are now "smartjeans,"

"Market Magic: Smart Jeans Can Save Your Life," by Andrea Castillo, Foundation for Economic Education, June 4, 2015. https://fee.org/articles/market-magic-smart-jeans-can -save-your-life/. Licensed under CC BY-4.0.

allowing you to interact with your phone and the Internet with a mere touch of the fabric.

The range of applications are numerous and subtle.

Take health monitoring, a market currently served by somewhat clunky armband devices. "Tactile computing" can be similarly used to monitor the wearer's health vitals, like her heart rate, blood pressure, sleep schedule, and even her mood—all without the added hassle of remembering to put on that easy-to-lose FitBit.

We could easily track our day-to-day health, identifying and changing the behaviors that are revealed to have undermined our wellness. If a wearer suffers a heart attack, the nearest hospital and his closest relatives could be immediately alerted. Health insurance premiums could be more precisely calibrated to reflect the underlying risk of each individual's lifestyle profile.

Such networked clothing could bring significant cost savings indeed, with researchers at McKinsey estimating that wearables could generate $1.1 trillion to $2.5 trillion in economic value by the year 2025.

Or consider the possibilities presented when wearable technologies begin interacting with other networked technologies.

My colleague Adam Thierer has written extensively on the "Internet of Things," an ecosystem of physical objects—vehicles, appliances, thermostats, lights, utilities, and consumer devices—that are embedded with microchips, sensors, and wireless communication capabilities to connect and autonomously interact with each other. These devices can be pre-programmed to communicate and dynamically adjust based on the feedback provided by other devices—all without requiring the user to lift a finger.

Life is more soothing when driven by data.

In the not-too-distant future, your phone's daily schedule will sync with your driverless car, picking you up from the office at the ideal time to minimize rush hour headaches.

Your health tracker, sensing elevated stress and low sugar levels, triggers your home devices to softly play your favorite music, dim the lights, and comfortably cool your surroundings.

Your oven is already heated by the time you get home, after consulting with your refrigerator about the optimal mix of self-ordered contents and designing a recipe for one of your favorite meals, of course.

"Smart" clothes can be integrated into this system to automate more tedious tasks and free up more of our time for the things that matter to us.

Sound far-fetched?

Check out Disney World, where wearable technologies are already making the Magic Kingdom a little more magic. A single unobtrusive rubber bracelet called the "MagicBand" wirelessly coordinates park access, reservations, payments, "FastPass" line-hopping privileges, meals, and even luggage transfer as if divined by a fairy godmother's enchanted wand.

Little girls dressed as princesses squeal in delight as they are greeted by name when they arrive for the tea in Cinderella's castle. Anonymized guest tracking reveals that crowds are swelling in Tomorrowland; a Frozen-themed parade is then queued to decongest the horde.

Fathers no longer need to fear crest-fallen faces if the meet-and-greet line for Mickey Mouse precludes some quality time with his children; with the MagicBand, families can securely reserve such priorities, which lessens stress and leaves more time to enjoy the new memories they are sharing.

As *Wired* explains, "The MagicBands, the thousands of sensors they talk to, and the 100 systems linked together to create MyMagicPlus turns the park into a giant computer." But your little brother doesn't see any of that: He just revels as he high-fives Buzz Lightyear.

While holographic fingernails excite and grab headlines, wearable technologies like Project Jacquard will secure true success when the improvements they bring to our lives are as unremarkable as instant navigation on our smartphones.

This marginal mundanity of magic is a testament to the market's drive to make our lives the most comfortable as possible while requiring from us the least possible exertion. Data-driven technologies allow us to drill down to granular market and non-market tastes alike, harnessing algorithms and data monitoring as a kind of emulated price signal that makes the best use of our own consumer information.

Just as networked technologies amplify the positive effects of markets, they can agitate skeptics' concerns.

As more decisions are automated away from human judgment into the background of data coordination, some will worry that technology designers hold an alarming degree of subtle control over their daily lives.

But these arguments are already made today about online data tracking; few who call for regulation actually read the data policies to which they agreed or cease using the technologies over which they agonize.

The same arguments made for markets today can be modified for the Internet of Things tomorrow: Where these technologies introduce vulnerabilities to security (in the case of hacking) or consumer safety, another market opportunity to add value presents itself.

Should consumers keep buying smart jeans, it will be a strong indicator that the market values data-driven fashion more than it fears Skynet-through-style. And one day, we'll look back and wonder how we ever got on without it.

CHAPTER 2

Is Increased IoT-Powered Automation a Good Thing?

Overview: How IoT Will Transform How Industries Function

Calum McClelland

Calum McClelland is the head of operations at IoT for All. He is deeply interested in the moral ramifications of new technologies and believes in leveraging the internet of things to help build a better world for everyone.

The Internet of Things is rife with acronyms, from LPWAN to MQTT to the acronym IoT itself. But if that wasn't enough, we also have several variations on IoT! One such variation is IIoT, which stands for the Industrial Internet of Things. So what's the difference between IoT and IIoT you ask? That's exactly what this post is about.

> Worldwide…a 1% improvement in industrial productivity could add $10 trillion to $15 trillion to worldwide GDP over the next 15 years.
>
> —Chunka Mui, *Forbes*

The Difference Between IoT and IIoT

In my previous #askIoT post, Internet of Things Examples and Applications, we saw that the Internet of Things (IoT) adds value in three major areas: increasing efficiency, improving health/safety, and creating better experiences. The Industrial Internet of Things deals with the first two areas, increasing efficiency and improving health/safety.

IIoT refers to a subcategory of the broader Internet of Things. IoT includes IIoT plus things like asset tracking, remote monitoring, wearables, and more. IIoT focuses specifically on industrial applications such as manufacturing or agriculture.

"What's the Difference Between IoT and IIoT (the Industrial Internet of Things)?" by Calum McClelland, IoT for All, January 6, 2019. Reprinted by permission.

The Massive Potential of IIoT

The Industrial Internet [of Things] will transform many industries, including manufacturing, oil and gas, agriculture, mining, transportation and healthcare. Collectively, these account for nearly two-thirds of the world economy.

—World Economic Forum, Industrial Internet of Things Report

In recent years, innovations in hardware, connectivity, big data analytics, and machine-learning have converged to generate huge opportunities for industries. Hardware innovations mean that sensors are cheaper, more powerful, and run longer on battery life. Connectivity innovations mean that it's cheaper and easier to send the data from these sensors to the cloud. Big data analytics and machine learning innovations mean that, once sensor data is collected, it's possible to gain incredible insight into manufacturing processes.

These insights can lead to massive increases in productivity and drastic reductions in cost. Whatever is being manufactured, it can be done faster, with fewer resources, and at a lower cost.

An example of the potential of IIoT is predictive maintenance. A broken machine in a manufacturing process can mean millions of dollars in lost productivity while production halts to fix the issue.

The past solution was to regularly scheduled maintenance, but this has a few issues. What if the machine breaks before the maintenance? This leads to a huge loss of productivity as described above. And what if the machine doesn't need maintenance? Time, effort, and money is wasted that could be better spent elsewhere.

Predictive maintenance means using more sensors to collect better data on machines, and then using data analytics and machine learning to determine exactly when a machine will need maintenance. Not too late, which leads to broken machines, and not too early, which leads to misallocated resources.

Predictive maintenance is just one example, and it's already a reality.

As adoption and advancement of IIoT accelerates, the changes will be profound. Eventually, we can achieve an autonomous economy in which supply exactly meets demand, completely optimizing the production process and leading to zero-waste.

And there's every reason to think that IIoT will accelerate in the near-term…

Adoption of IIoT

In many ways, IIoT is ahead of IoT, and will continue to see faster adoption. Why? A key difference between IoT and IIoT is that, unlike consumer IoT applications, incentives for adopting IIoT technologies are much greater:

> [IoT and IIoT have] two distinctly separate areas of interest. The Industrial IoT connects critical machines and sensors in high-stakes industries such as aerospace and defense, healthcare and energy. These are systems in which failure often results in life-threatening or other emergency situations. On the other hand, IoT systems tend to be consumer-level devices such as wearable fitness tools, smart home thermometers and automatic pet feeders. They are important and convenient, but breakdowns do not immediately create emergency situations.
>
> — RTI

Another difference between IoT and IIoT is that there are clearer near-term benefits for IIoT vs IoT. Manufacturing companies can reduce costs and increase productivity, meaning more tangible return-on-investment for adopting IIoT solutions. Companies like ThyssenKrupp, Caterpillar, and Thames Water are already reaping benefits from being early IIoT adopters.

But IIoT isn't without its challenges…

Barriers to IIoT

Two of the biggest hurdles are security and interoperability.

Bringing physical systems online generates substantial benefits, but also means that those systems can be potentially compromised.

Cyberattacks become scary when they can enable remote control of or damage to physical systems; huge financial losses at best and serious injuries or death at worst. Security is a major concern for IoT in general and needs to be a big part of the conversation in the coming years.

To collect the data from sensors and make that data useful, everything in the system needs to work together. Lack of interoperability and lack of standards between IoT sensors, devices, connectivity, and communication protocols can hinder the process of connecting everything. This is also a problem for IoT in general.

Considering the Implications of IIoT

> In 1980, it took 25 jobs to generate $1 million in manufacturing output in the US. Today, it takes just 6.5 jobs to generate that amount.
>
> —Brookings

As we head into the future and see accelerated IIoT adoption, the increases in productivity will be even more pronounced. Tesla's Gigafactory will be highly automated, promising a staggering $100 billion in output with only 6,500 workers. That's only 1.3 jobs to generate $1 million in manufacturing output.

So what does this mean for US jobs?

On the positive side, this will likely help bring manufacturing back into the US from abroad. Manufacturing moved outside of the US because labor was cheaper in foreign countries, but IIoT solutions will create machines and systems that outcompete this cheap manual labor.

IIoT will also create entirely new industries and categories of jobs to support these high-tech systems. Medical robot designers, grid modernization managers, intermodal transportation network engineers, and more.

However, we should be wary that there may be fewer jobs created than destroyed. As shown above, increases in productivity mean fewer jobs are needed to create the same value, potentially meaning fewer jobs overall.

And even if there is no net job-loss or even a net job-gain, we also need to consider the kinds of jobs being created and destroyed. The new job categories will demand interdisciplinary skills; deep knowledge about specific industries coupled with skills and expertise in new technologies, software, data analytics, system integration, and cybersecurity.

These jobs are not blue-collar, the skills will take high-level training and education. How will this training and education be provided? Who's going to pay for it? I don't have answers, but these questions are critical to consider as we head into our next Industrial Revolution.

IoT-Powered Automation Will Change Commerce

Kayla Matthews

Kayla Matthews is a tech journalist and writer who focuses on AI, robotics, and smart homes for a publication called the IoT Times.

Some of the current applications of the Internet of Things feel more trivial than others. Humans have been outrunning each other for a hundred thousand years without the aid of internet-connected sneakers, for instance. And using telephones to close the blinds in our homes often feels like more, not less, work.

But commercial IoT is a different beast. It's distinct from consumer IoT and arrives with different challenges and a separate set of benefits and opportunities. Here's a look at five of them.

1. Make Your Buildings More Efficient

Optimizing and automating building functionality—including HVAC and lighting—is one of the first and most appealing steps a company can make to take advantage of commercial IoT.

Internet-connected company infrastructure can take a page out of the consumer IoT playbook by creating separate profiles for each part of a building, based on the habits and preferences of the people who usually occupy it.

A company headquarters with multiple floors and teams won't have the same environmental requirements for each department—and after learning about typical usage, IoT devices like smart thermostats and smart humidity controls don't even need to be programmed by the end customer. They'll turn on when needed to the ideal temperature and reduce the temperature later when that part of the building is unoccupied again.

"5 Benefits of Commercial IoT and Automation," by Kayla Matthews, IoT for All, May 30, 2019. Reprinted by permission.

The same concept applies to automating facility and campus lighting systems as well. Unoccupied rooms won't burn through your utility budget. Instead, IoT solutions can dim or turn off the lighting automatically.

2. Bring Intelligence to the Supply Chain and Asset Management

Supply chain management goes far beyond estimating the time of arrival for a shipment of finished goods or raw materials. Thanks to advancements in sensors and scanning technologies, companies can perform ongoing cycle counts as products roll off the assembly floor using tracker tags (e.g. RFID) in the field, including vehicles and other equipment (e.g. with GPS).

Passive RFID improves on existing inventory and asset management technologies, such as barcodes, because they require less manual intervention. No matter what kinds of products or assets pass through your doors or loading docks—be they delivery vehicles, computers, furniture, or heavy equipment—keeping track of them in real-time, from destination to origin, is easier now than it ever was.

3. Improve Customer Insights and Boost Conversion

Sensors and location beacons in retail businesses and other commercial locations can yield valuable insights for the company and make life easier for the customer at the same time. On the consumer side of things, location-based technologies offer opportunities like these:

- Geofencing delivers personalized recommendations and discounts when customers make an appearance in a brick-and-mortar store.
- Location beacons can provide walking directions to help navigate to a desired product or area of the building.

The insights delivered by location and geofencing technologies unlock huge potential for businesses as well. By gathering data about how customers move around a retail space and which areas see the most traffic, companies can make better decisions about layout, inventory and product promotions. Those insights can also offer information about which types of customers frequent a location at various times of day and throughout the year.

Another concept, sometimes called "geoconquesting," uses geofencing to deliver offers to customers who pass close to a competitor location. When Dunkin Donuts rolled out a geoconquesting campaign based on competitor locations, they found that 36 percent of the customers who received the offer took them up on it.

4. Boost Safety Compliance and Facilitate Real-Time Decisions

Commercial IoT can be an ally when it comes to compliance and customer safety.

For companies that trade in perishable goods—whether a retail entity or a supply chain company tasked with safe delivery—the FDA provides regulations for temperature thresholds and the maximum time that products may exceed them. Refrigerated food products aren't fit for sale after two hours in temperatures exceeding 40°F. As a result, companies need something more than a temperature gauge. They need wireless connectivity providing awareness of things like refrigerated truck delays, power losses (even brief ones) and other factors that might put their compliance—and their customers—at risk.

Commercial IoT delivers such tools in the form of remote temperature probes and cloud connectivity for immediate (and auditable) data trails. The ability to observe data in real-time and make more timely decisions can help risk-averse companies save face as well as money. Food recalls jumped by an incredible 92 percent between 2012 and 2017 in the US alone. Reacting in a timely fashion to quality control issues could help avoid a recall—or greatly cut down on reaction time if one proves necessary.

5. Improve Workplace Safety and Access Control

There are many ways IoT can facilitate workplace safety.

Assets equipped with sensors can alert maintenance staff proactively about impending parts failures to avoid employee injury. Connected technology can also automatically grant or restrict access to parts of a facility based on which employees are authorized and which are not. In 2017, over 4,000 deaths resulted from preventable circumstances—and preventive maintenance and access control are two keys for bringing that number down.

Access control can be a big cybersecurity problem. Many companies take the end-to-end security of their data pipelines for granted. And that's a mistake since the average data breach can cost a small business an average of $120,000 for each incident.

With IoT powering automated security gates and doors and employees using wearables or badges, your building's security system can recognize the approach of employees and unlock doors to facilities of high-risk areas and then lock them again afterward, or even grant and restrict privileges for operating certain machinery.

As we can see here, the implications for the Internet of Things in the commercial world are even more compelling than those at the consumer level. They can add real value to an organization and help tackle longstanding problems, including efficiency, compliance, safety, customer engagement and much more.

The Internet of Things Plugs In Communities of Color

Nicol Turner Lee

Nicol Turner Lee is a senior fellow at the Brookings Institution, a Washington, DC, think tank.

More than 500 billion IoT devices, from sensors, to actuators, to medical devices, will be connected to the internet by 2030, according to research from Cisco.[1] The data collected, aggregated, and analyzed by IoT devices will deliver insights across a wide variety of platforms and services, from health care to artificial intelligence innovations. 5G networks will be needed to meet the requirements of these data-intensive IoT devices and related cloud services.

Nationwide, resilient 5G networks will also be needed to accommodate the growing demand for high-speed mobile broadband. While some researchers and analysts suggest that existing 4G Long-Term Evolution (LTE) technology is sufficient for the majority of IoT use cases, this paper argues that only high-speed, high-capacity, low-latency 5G broadband networks will meet the demands of data-intensive applications. High-capacity and high-throughput operations will also be supported through 5G networks, making scaled IoT deployments even more cost effective. As 5G and IoT are broadly applied to life-saving devices and applications in the areas of health care, energy and transportation, it is imperative that they operate as anticipated, without fail, every time.

Further, access to 5G networks will be a determining factor in whether or not mobile-dependent users fully partake in the digital economy, especially as smartphones, cell phones, or other wireless-enabled devices have become their only gateway to the

"Enabling Opportunities: 5G, the Internet of Things, and Communities of Color," by Nicol Turner Lee, The Brookings Institution, January 9, 2019. Reprinted by permission.

internet. Currently, 95 percent of Americans own a cell phone and 77 percent have smartphones, according to the Pew Research Center.[2] Ownership cuts across demographic groups with African-Americans and Hispanics showing high levels of mobile device ownership. For low-income segments of these populations, wireless connectivity is most likely their only online access.

While IoT and related applications are just one of many use cases powered by next-generation mobile networks, I argue that they offer the most promise for eliminating the disadvantages resulting from the digital divide, especially for certain segments of African-Americans and Hispanics who are severely marginalized or socially isolated. Exploring the relationship between 5G and IoT by drawing upon existing use cases, this paper makes the case for why the United States needs nationwide 5G networks to leverage access to both services and opportunities for these populations.

[…]

Broadband Access for Communities of Color

Twenty-four million Americans lack access to fixed, residential high-speed broadband services, according to 2018 data from the Federal Communications Commission (FCC).[4] This includes 13 percent of African-Americans, 11 percent of Hispanics, 35 percent of those lacking a high school degree, 22 percent of rural residents, and 37.2 percent of households that speak limited English.[5] In this accounting for differences in income, age, education and other factors, many racial and ethnic groups also continue to lag behind whites in residential broadband adoption.

Despite these disparities, mobile access has converged among many of these subgroups. Seventy-seven percent of whites, 75 percent of African-Americans, and 77 percent of Hispanics own a smartphone, according to the Pew Research Center.[6] For many higher-income whites, access to the internet via a smartphone supplements a high-speed, in-home broadband connection, while lower-income populations, less-educated, and younger Americans tend to be more smartphone-dependent, relying on mobile broadband as their primary and oftentimes sole connection to the internet.[7] Further, 35 percent of Hispanics and 24 percent of African-Americans have no other online connection except through their smartphones or other mobile devices, compared to 14 percent of whites.[8] Thirty-one percent of individuals making less than $30,000 per year regularly rely on their mobile device for internet access.[9] Finally, urban residents also tend to be more smartphone-dependent at 22 percent compared to 17 percent of rural and suburban residents.

Many of these smartphone-dependent populations overlap with those impacted by higher rates of unemployment, disparate educational attainment and limited economic mobility. For example, unemployed and under-employed African-Americans may face challenges in meeting current workforce demands due to limited digital skills, training, and access to online job openings. Despite advances in education since the 1970s, African-Americans experience higher rates of unemployment, potentially attributed to the lack of digital access in an information-rich economy.

[...]

IoT Use Cases and People of Color

Not surprising, IoT can be optimized on next-generation mobile networks. By definition, IoT refers to physical things connected to each other using wireless communications services.[13] As a global data infrastructure, IoT devices will generate massive amounts of data, which can be used to streamline and improve a wide variety of services and industries. 5G will be an important input for IoT, especially for devices and applications that require high reliability, strong security, widespread availability, and in some cases, ultra-low latency.

Because 5G's technical features can simultaneously support massive numbers of devices, certain segments of African-American and Hispanic populations may be able to access services that are insufficiently available in certain urban and rural communities.

When applied to the verticals of health care, education, energy use, and transportation, IoT can reduce the cost of service delivery, make more accurate decisions around outputs (including costs), and empower consumers around individual and community concerns. Many of the advanced technologies will be promising for more isolated and mobile-dependent populations, potentially solving some of their challenges. The remainder of this section describes these IoT use cases more generally.

Health Care

In the US, one-in-two American adults suffer from a chronic disease, while one-in-four American adults have multiple chronic diseases.[14] Compared to whites, people of color are disproportionately affected by a range of chronic diseases, especially heart disease and diabetes. For example, between 2011 and 2014, African-Americans were more likely to be afflicted by diabetes than whites (18 percent compared to 9.6 percent).[15] Forty percent of African-Americans are also more likely to have high blood pressure with very little management and control of its treatment.

The life expectancy at birth for African-Americans, 75 years, is four years lower than for whites.[16] For African-Americans in particular, IoT has the potential to facilitate remote diagnosis, foster adherence to prescribed interventions and medications, and assist in the administration of medical services, including appointment scheduling, insurance management, and treatment plans. For example:

- Home health sensing, a critical intervention for chronic disease patients, uses the microphones in smartphones to replicate spirometers, which measure air flow in and out of lungs for patients with chronic obstructive pulmonary disease (COPD). The data collected is used by doctors to monitor the disease's progression in patients in real-time.
- Novartis, Qualcomm, and Propeller Health are also tackling COPD by connecting an inhaler device to a digital platform via a sensor that passively records and transmits usage data for patients.

- Proteus Digital Health has developed ingestible sensors that aid in treatment adherence. This sensor generates a signal after medicine is taken, which relays the data to a smartphone application and eventually to the medical provider.[17]

In these examples, having the ability to transmit results to health care providers means fewer trips to the hospital and improved health monitoring for patients. While data is not available on how African-Americans and Hispanics are specifically engaging these IoT applications, it is worth noting that each of these innovations are attempting to remedy the health care gaps caused by the physical or social isolation of patients. When matched with the historical data on certain chronic diseases affecting African-Americans and Hispanics, IoT health care applications can help address the disparate conditions that restrict access to primary and supportive patient care. Next-generation mobile networks can also spur the development of other emerging health care devices and applications.

Education

Historically, students of color have faced persistent educational disparities that unfortunately reflect differences in their socioeconomic status. While educational gaps have narrowed between whites and people of color on fourth and eighth grade math tests and fourth grade reading tests (benchmarks for student performance), African-Americans have lagged behind whites and Hispanics in educational attainment.[18] Further, three-fourths of minority students attend schools where a majority of their classmates qualifies as poor or low-income compared to one-third of whites.[19]

These statistics, coupled with the "homework gap," or the barriers that students face when they don't have broadband at home, further stifle educational attainment for disadvantaged populations. Data from my national survey shows that use of the internet for homework is lowest among Hispanic (2.4 percent) and African-American (2.5 percent) respondents, which could be attributed to an insufficient or non-existent broadband connection.

Universal service programs, such as Lifeline and E-Rate, can help to alleviate some of the barriers to low-income broadband adoption, but they are not wholly sustainable by themselves to level the playing field for students of color.[20]

In line with the argument in this paper, IoT educational solutions can potentially contribute to more vibrant and robust school learning environments, including:

- Interactive whiteboards;
- eBooks;
- Tablets and mobile devices;
- 3-D printers;
- Student ID cards; and,
- Student tracking systems.[21]

IoT can also personalize the learning experience for students by tailoring lessons to the student's pace and style of learning, and capturing more data about the factors that boost their performance with every lesson.[22] One such application is the result of IBM's partnership with the textbook publisher Pearson to create software that allows students to ask questions, provides helpful feedback to the student, and keeps instructors updated on student progress.[23] But, these applications and others require high-bandwidth connections, which are often not available or consistent in lower-income neighborhoods.

IoT technologies can also expand the possibilities for what and where students learn. Leveraging IoT, students of color can collaborate with each other and teachers in real time regardless of distance.[24] For example, using virtual reality headsets, students in remote locations can place themselves in a classroom with their peers or transport teachers and students anywhere in the world (or universe) that the curriculum takes them, from inside the human body to the far reaches of the solar system.[25] For students of color in less digitally connected schools, these technologies can make a marked difference in educational outcomes.

In addition to these classroom possibilities, some schools are also engaging IoT applications to:

- Embed RFID chips in ID cards to track the presence of students, enabling tracking of tardiness and absenteeism and logging of students' presence on campus.[26]
- Deploy GPS-enabled bus systems where routes can be tracked so parents and administrators know where a given bus is at any time. Students can also be notified when the bus is near their pickup location to avoid long waits.
- Activate wireless key lock systems in classrooms to ensure student safety.

While these applications can operate over today's 4G LTE networks, the affordability, scalability, and accessibility of 5G is projected to make these tools even more effective and precise.

[…]

Endnotes

1. Cisco. 2016. "Internet of Things." https://www.cisco.com/c/dam/en/us/products /collateral/se/internet-of things/at-a-glance-c45-731471.pdf.

2. "Mobile Fact Sheet." 2018. Washington, DC: Pew Research Center, February 5, 2018. www.pewinternet.org/fact sheet/mobile.

4. "2018 Broadband Deployment Report." 2018. Washington, DC: Federal Communications Commission, February 5, 2018. https://www.fcc.gov/reports -research/reports/broadband-progress-reports/2018-broadband-deployment-report.

5. Ryan, Camille. 2018. "Computer and Internet Use in the United States: 2016." US Census: American Community Survey Reports, August 2018. https://www.census .gov/library/publications/2018/acs/acs-39.html. See also: Anderson, Monica, Andrew Perrin, and Jingjing Jiang. 2018. "11% of Americans Don't Use the Internet. Who Are They?" Fact Tank (blog), Washington, DC: Pew Research Center, March 5, 2018. http://www.pewresearch.org/fact-tank/2018/03/05/some-americans-dont-use -the-internet-who-are-they/. Anderson, Monica, and Andrew Perrin. 2017. "Disabled Americans Less Likely to Use Technology." Fact Tank (blog), Washington, DC: Pew Research Center, April 7, 2017. http://www.pewresearch.org/fact -tank/2017/04/07/disabled-americans-are-less-likely-to-use-technology/.

6. "Mobile Fact Sheet." 2018. Washington, DC: Pew Research Center, February 5, 2018. http://www.pewinternet.org/fact-sheet/mobile/.

7. Ibid.

8. "Internet/Broadband Fact Sheet." 2018. Washington, DC: Pew Research Center, February 5, 2018. www.pewinternet.org/fact-sheet/internet-broadband.

9. Ibid.

13. Popescul, Daniela, and Mircea Georgescu. "Internet of Things—Some Ethical Issues." The USV Annals of Economics and Public Administration 13, no. 2 (18) (2013). http://seap.usv.ro/annals/ojs/index.php/annals/article/viewFile/628/599.

14. Centers for Disease Control and Prevention. "Chronic Diseases in America." Fact Sheet. https://www.cdc.gov/chronicdisease/resources/infographic/chronic-diseases.html.

15. Centers for Disease Control and Prevention. "Racial and Ethnic Approaches to Community Health." Fact Sheet. https://www.cdc.gov/chronicdisease/resources/publications/aag/pdf/2016/reach-aag.pdf.

16. Arias, Elizabeth, Melonie Heron, and Jiaquan Xu. 2017. "United States Life Tables, 2014." National Vital Statistics Report 66, no. 4 (August 14, 2017): 64.

17. "Adherence to Long-Term Therapies." Washington, DC: World Health Organization, 2013. http://apps.who.int/iris/bitstream/handle/10665/42682/9241545992.pdf.

18. "Indicator 6: Elementary and Secondary Enrollment." 2017. National Center for Education Statistics. July 2017. https://nces.ed.gov/programs/raceindicators/indicator_rbb.asp.

19. "The Condition of Education—Preprimary, Elementary, and Secondary Education—Schools—Concentration of Public School Students Eligible for Free or Reduced-Price Lunch—Indicator March (2018)." National Center for Education Statistics. March 2018. https://nces.ed.gov/programs/coe/indicator_clb.asp.

20. "E-Rate: Universal Service Program for Schools and Libraries." 2011. Federal Communications Commission. May 24, 2011. https://www.fcc.gov/consumers/guides/universal-service-program-schools-and-libraries-e-rate.

21. "IoT in the Classroom: How Traditional Education Is Changing." Aldridge. August 17, 2016. https://aldridge.com/future-iot-in-the-classroom-education/.

22. Leligou, Helen C., Emmnouil Zacharioudakis, Louisa Bouta, and Evangelos Niokos. 2017. "5G technologies boosting efficient mobile learning." MATEC Web of Conferences, vol. 125, p. 03004. EDP Sciences, 2017.

23. "IBM and Pearson to Drive Cognitive Learning Experiences for College Students." 2016. IBM News Room. October 25, 2016. https://www-03.ibm.com/press/us/en/pressrelease/50842.wss.

24. Leligou, Helen C., Emmnouil Zacharioudakis, Louisa Bouta, and Evangelos Niokos. 2017. "5G technologies boosting efficient mobile learning." MATEC Web of Conferences, vol. 125, p. 03004. EDP Sciences, 2017.

25. Mirzamany, Esmat, Adrian Neal, Mischa Dohler, and Maria Lema Rosas. "5G and Education." Bristol, United Kingdom: Jisc, n.d. https://community.jisc.ac.uk/sites/default/files/Education-VM_Extended.pdf.

26. Kravets, David. 2012. "Tracking School Children with RFID Tags? It's All About the Benjamins." Wired, September 7, 2012. https://www.wired.com/2012/09/rfid-chip-student-monitoring/.

The Internet of Things Changes Whom Workplaces Work For

Kayla Matthews

Kayla Matthews is a tech journalist and writer who focuses on AI, robotics, and smart homes for a publication called the IoT Times.

Major changes that affect the workplace tend to cause mixed emotions. That's true in the case of the Internet of Things (IoT) and the connected devices under its umbrella.

Will high-tech advances make your life easier? Or will smart devices make your job obsolete?

Let's take a look at some of the most likely ways the IoT will alter things at work and explore the pros and cons of such developments.

How the IoT Will Affect Your Job

1. The Reduction of Repetitive Tasks

One of the positive aspects of the IoT on employees is that it'll probably mimic the assembly line by reducing repetition in the work environment, especially when the IoT devices learn from past experiences.

From that point on, the humans who used to handle those jobs can spend more of their time on rewarding and mentally challenging work.

Think about how some repetitive tasks, such as typing, can cause problems like carpal tunnel syndrome (though this is rare). Still, severe cases require surgery and may make a person who types a lot for a living unable to work as efficiently.

However, many IoT devices recognize voice commands, theoretically allowing people to type less and talk more.

"How the IoT Will Affect Your Job," by Kayla Matthews, Softonic International S.A., April 11, 2018. Reprinted by permission.

2. Less Employee Autonomy

There's also a possibility that the IoT will adversely affect your ability to make some decisions, mostly because as devices try to deliver convenience, they may make it so that you don't have to choose.

Consider an IoT-enabled coffee maker that learns what time you get to work and has your favorite brew waiting when you arrive. Or what about a thermostat that knows you like to drop the temperature by a few degrees in your office each afternoon to help yourself stay alert? Both of these examples already exist, and they'll become even more prominent in workplaces, as well as homes.

Although you can change settings so that the gadgets don't keep doing things that don't suit your preferences, the fact that the smart devices know what you want before you ask may make you feel stripped of free will.

3. Better Data Collection

As mentioned above, IoT gadgets that help humans take care of tedious work could give them more time to do other things. Those devices can also capture data that accumulates during workdays, allowing managers to analyze that information and make wiser decisions.

According to some estimates, it's possible to process up to 90 percent of invoices without human intervention. That statistic shows how automation could drastically affect the workforce of the future.

Because processing data is only one part of the equation, some companies offer platforms help business leaders see all of them with one interface.

The Google Cloud IoT Core service provides users with the infrastructures and services necessary to manage numerous connected devices at once, thereby facilitating better data usage over time.

When managers efficiently use those gadgets and the information they compile over time, it should be easier to make profitable choices, increase employee productivity and create an all-around better work environment.

4. The Possibility of Unintended Career Changes

It's not difficult to find alarmist articles about how the IoT and related technologies could steal jobs.

According to one study carried out by Harvard academics, 47 percent of US jobs are in the "high risk" category for being replaced by automation.

However, it's important to realize how the IoT is also creating jobs people hadn't previously imagined. That's happening inside and outside the United States. For example, Aruna Sundararajan, a government telecommunications leader in India, believes the IoT will create up to 15 million new jobs in the country over the next few years.

Instead of thinking the worst and assuming the IoT might make you unemployed, now is the time to prepare for what's ahead and gain the knowledge needed to start working in an IoT-centric role potentially.

Depending on factors such as your age, the field in which you work and how much you like your job, you might have thought you'd stay in your current position until retirement.

Shifting into a different role might seem scary at first because you're making a move you hadn't planned for.

However, the specialization required by many IoT jobs means they also offer higher-than-average salaries. Even if you hadn't thought of changing careers, your decision to do so—or at least keep the option in mind—could help your career and boost your bank account balance.

Pros and Cons

Based on this list, you can see there are pros and cons associated with the growing prevalence of the IoT in today's workplaces.

In the best-case scenario, employers should take their workers' concerns into account when implementing emerging IoT technologies, while workers should stay continually alert for ways to develop their skills in case a career change becomes the best option.

The Internet of Things Has Created an Ad World

Joshua A. T. Fairfield

Joshua Fairfield writes about law and technology and teaches at Washington and Lee University School of Law.

Internet-enabled devices are so common, and so vulnerable, that hackers recently broke into a casino through its fish tank. The tank had internet-connected sensors measuring its temperature and cleanliness. The hackers got into the fish tank's sensors and then to the computer used to control them, and from there to other parts of the casino's network. The intruders were able to copy 10 gigabytes of data to somewhere in Finland.

By gazing into this fish tank, we can see the problem with "internet of things" devices: We don't really control them. And it's not always clear who does—though often software designers and advertisers are involved.

In my recent book, *Owned: Property, Privacy and the New Digital Serfdom*, I discuss what it means that our environment is seeded with more sensors than ever before. Our fish tanks, smart televisions, internet-enabled home thermostats, Fitbits and smartphones constantly gather information about us and our environment. That information is valuable not just for us but for people who want to sell us things. They ensure that internet-enabled devices are programmed to be quite eager to share information.

Take, for example, Roomba, the adorable robotic vacuum cleaner. Since 2015, the high-end models have created maps of its users' homes, to more efficiently navigate through them while cleaning. But as Reuters and Gizmodo reported recently, Roomba's manufacturer, iRobot, may plan to share those maps of the layouts of people's private homes with its commercial partners.

Security and Privacy Breaches Are Built In

Like the Roomba, other smart devices can be programmed to share our private information with advertisers over back-channels of which we are not aware. In a case even more intimate than the Roomba business plan, a smartphone-controllable erotic massage device, called WeVibe, gathered information about how often, with what settings and at what times of day it was used. The WeVibe app sent that data back to its manufacturer—which agreed to pay a multi-million-dollar legal settlement when customers found out and objected to the invasion of privacy.

Those back-channels are also a serious security weakness. The computer manufacturer Lenovo, for instance, used to sell its computers with a program called "Superfish" preinstalled. The program was intended to allow Lenovo—or companies that paid it—to secretly insert targeted advertisements into the results of users' web searches. The way it did so was downright dangerous: It hijacked web browsers' traffic without the user's knowledge—including web communications users thought were securely encrypted, like connections to banks and online stores for financial transactions.

The Underlying Problem Is Ownership

One key reason we don't control our devices is that the companies that make them seem to think—and definitely act like—they still own them, even after we've bought them. A person may purchase a nice-looking box full of electronics that can function as a smartphone, the corporate argument goes, but they buy a license only to use the software inside. The companies say they still own the software, and because they own it, they can control it. It's as if a car dealer sold a car, but claimed ownership of the motor.

This sort of arrangement is destroying the concept of basic property ownership. John Deere has already told farmers that they don't really own their tractors but just license the software—so they can't fix their own farm equipment or even take it to an independent repair shop. The farmers are objecting, but maybe some people are willing to let things slide when it comes to smartphones, which are often bought on a payment installment plan and traded in as soon as possible.

How long will it be before we realize they're trying to apply the same rules to our smart homes, smart televisions in our living rooms and bedrooms, smart toilets and internet-enabled cars?

A Return to Feudalism?

The issue of who gets to control property has a long history. In the feudal system of medieval Europe, the king owned almost everything, and everyone else's property rights depended on their relationship with the king. Peasants lived on land granted by the king to a local lord, and workers didn't always even own the tools they used for farming or other trades like carpentry and blacksmithing.

Over the centuries, Western economies and legal systems evolved into our modern commercial arrangement: People and private companies often buy and sell items themselves and own land, tools and other objects outright. Apart from a few basic government rules like environmental protection and public health, ownership comes with no trailing strings attached.

This system means that a car company can't stop me from painting my car a shocking shade of pink or from getting the oil changed at whatever repair shop I choose. I can even try to modify or fix my car myself. The same is true for my television, my farm equipment and my refrigerator.

Yet the expansion of the internet of things seems to be bringing us back to something like that old feudal model, where people didn't own the items they used every day. In this 21st-century version, companies are using intellectual property law—intended to protect ideas—to control physical objects consumers think they own.

Intellectual Property Control

My phone is a Samsung Galaxy. Google controls the operating system and the Google Apps that make an Android smartphone work well. Google licenses them to Samsung, which makes its own modification to the Android interface, and sublicenses the right to use my own phone to me—or at least that is the argument that Google and Samsung make. Samsung cuts deals with lots of software providers which want to take my data for their own use.

But this model is flawed, in my view. We need the right to fix our own property. We need the right to kick invasive advertisers out of our devices. We need the ability to shut down the information back-channels to advertisers, not merely because we don't love being spied on, but because those back doors are security risks, as the stories of Superfish and the hacked fish tank show. If we don't have the right to control our own property, we don't really own it. We are just digital peasants, using the things that we have bought and paid for at the whim of our digital lord.

Even though things look grim right now, there is hope. These problems quickly become public relations nightmares for the companies involved. And there is serious bipartisan support for right-to-repair bills that restore some powers of ownership to consumers.

Recent years have seen progress in reclaiming ownership from would-be digital barons. What is important is that we recognize and reject what these companies are trying to do, buy accordingly, vigorously exercise our rights to use, repair and modify our smart property, and support efforts to strengthen those rights. The idea of property is still powerful in our cultural imagination, and it won't die easily. That gives us a window of opportunity. I hope we will take it.

Regulatory Constraints on Fiber Will Inhibit the Development of Smart Cities

Lauren McCarthy

Lauren McCarthy is a scholar of the urban realm, transportation, and the local policy process. She is program manager and researcher for the Center for Transportation for Public-Private Partnership Policy at George Mason University.

A cross the US, there are over 130,000 miles of bundled fiber optic cable, yet a good portion of these strands are "dark," or unused. There are a few reasons for this. First, the cost of subterranean installation is high, therefore excess strands were added to hedge against future demand. Second, following the dot-com bubble, many early fiber providers went bankrupt, leaving behind dormant fiber. Third, dark fiber is often installed purposely in anticipation of future technologies and uses, such as smart cities developed around the internet of things.

Dark fiber is a contentious issue, as the public and private sectors struggle to find a balanced policy approach to building it and lighting it up. Both sectors face considerable regulatory constraints, yet counterintuitively, the public sector is also imposing constraints upon itself. Municipal governments are often the target of state-level legislation that limits municipal build-out of fiber. Given the potential of internet access to positively impact education, health, and economic growth, it is in the public interest to undo these restrictions and to expand existing fiber capacity in an inclusive and equitable way.

"Enabling the Smart City—How Can the Public Sector Light Up Dark Fiber?" by Lauren McCarthy, Niskanen Center, September 3, 2019. https://www.niskanencenter.org /enabling-the-smart-city-how-can-the-public-sector-light-up-dark-fiber/. Licensed under CC BY-4.0 International.

Dark Fiber's Origins

The development of the laser beam enabled fiber optic networks to become a reality. Lasers, conveying pulses of light at different wavelengths along glass fibers, made fiber optic networks the gold standard in communication transmissions. One of the first experimental fiber optic cable systems was installed by AT&T in Atlanta in 1976. The following year AT&T installed a fiber optic cable system for commercial communications in Chicago. Additional commercial lines quickly followed, dramatically cutting the costs of telecommunication. At the same time, fiber optics were laid to create the "backbone of the internet" across the ocean floor and underneath countries and continents, ultimately connecting the world faster than ever before.

To connect residential and commercial buildings to the internet, fiber owners sell access to internet service providers (ISPs). ISPs then connect customers through slower but less expensive phone, cable, DSL, and wireless hookups, addressing the so-called "last mile problem." Due to the high costs associated with connecting residences, lower-than-expected demand, and recessionary market conditions in the 2000s, much of the US remains underserved by fiber—only 25 percent of consumers have direct access to a fiber optic network.

The projected data demands of the smart city have placed a spotlight on the lack of direct access to fiber networks in the US. Without a fiber network, the realization of a 5G next-generation mobile broadband network is near to impossible. In addition, internet connectivity is frequently being considered "critical infrastructure" by city governments. As a result, municipalities have grown hungry for access to more fiber—and dark fiber has become the object of intense policy debate.

The Impact of Anti-Municipal Broadband Legislation on Dark Fiber

To preserve the incumbent power long enjoyed by the private sector, lobbying efforts continue to promote anti-municipal-broadband policy. According to broadbandnow.com, in 2018 there were 20 states with laws restricting municipal broadband, rising to 26 states in 2019. The failure of proposed federal legislation intended to dissolve and prevent anti-municipal-broadband policies has reinforced these lobbying efforts. Private networks in urban areas often deliver fast, reliable connections, but rural, low-density suburban, and low-income urban areas are often underserved. Limiting municipal involvement in fiber networks has thus reduced equitable access to high-speed internet.

Restrictions placed on municipalities limit existing dark fiber utilization and development of new networks. These restrictions include bureaucratic complexities, referendum requirements, population caps for public networks, the use of public monies to only fund private or public-private deals, and other forms of private sector preference. In some states, for example, if a private sector company enters the market, the public network must cease operations and sell itself to the private provider. One might think this would be beneficial, leading to better service and higher speeds. Yet in some cases, such as that of Pinetops, North Carolina, the level of service and speed decreased with the introduction of a privately controlled network.

That said, the anti-municipal legislation, while restrictive, is not the death knell for municipalities seeking to leverage existing dark fiber or build new to enable local fiber networks. Many communities have built local government fiber networks. There are now 500 municipal networks and 300 cooperative sacross the country and the number continues to grow. A few methods have proven effective for delivering service to underserved communities and preparing for the smart city despite the restrictions.

1) Regional Cooperation Utilizing Economies of Scale
Three sections of the Virginia code (VA Code § 56-265.4:4; VA Code § 56-484.7:1; VA Code § 15.2-2108.6) place bureaucratic barriers on the deployment of municipal networks. Nonetheless, five cities in Virginia have banded together to create a 100-mile

open-access dark fiber connectivity ring around Hampton Roads. These cities are purposely putting in excess capacity to accommodate future smart city demand. Funding and financing for the project has been obtained from a variety of sources, including grants, awards, and private equity and debt. Leveraging public-private partnerships and regional collaboration, a commission has engaged with academic institutions, technology companies, and state organizations to create a master plan and coordinate the network. The dark fiber network is intended to be able to connect the entire region through command centers that will coordinate the management of the data.

2) Cooperatives

Cooperatives are popular options for rural areas restricted by municipal broadband laws. The need for one such network in Cook County, Minnesota, resulted in the formation of a co-op between Arrowhead Electric Company (AEC) and True North Broadband. The county supported the project through grants, along with federal grants and loans. As a result, by linking into existing dark fiber and expanding the network, the co-op has connected around 5,500 households and businesses that previously relied on satellite or cellular data for connectivity. In addition to creating the co-op, AEC recognized that as a primarily electric company, it has broadband technical deficiencies and partnered with the Consolidated Telecommunications Company to handle service calls AEC cannot handle itself. Unfortunately, the biggest protection these communities have against the regulations are that they are simply too small for large telecoms to invest in. It would seem these would be the communities most vulnerable to cost overruns and mismanagement, and yet they are leveraging local assets and knowledge to effectively building out rural networks.

3) Buyback of Private Networks for Government-Only Use

Some states, such as Pennsylvania, flatly bar municipalities from selling fiber optic service to consumers. This means a local municipality can build its own network for government use only.

Philadelphia attempted to build a public broadband network in the early 2000s with the intent of providing public Wi-Fi. Though it sought private partners to build the network, the city faced considerable pushback from incumbent companies. The telecom companies, rather than place a bid, elected to campaign against the project. This has led to a legacy of private incumbent companies pushing for greater restrictions on public service. Philadelphia ultimately did build its own network, but had to sell it to the private sector once restrictive legislation was passed in 2005. Recently, the city was able to buy the network back from the private sector and it is now using previously dark fiber to connect government services.

Lighting Up Dark Fiber Without Restrictive Legislation: The Case of Maryland

Maryland is a state without restrictive legislation and offers a model for states not burdened under excessive regulation. Maryland has developed a 1,294-mile broadband network by connecting three existing networks: network Maryland, Inter-County Broadband N network (ICBN), and Maryland Broadband Cooperative (MDBC). The network first connects government and anchor institutions to offer service to underserved and unserved areas alongside privately delivered networks. The connection of the three networks evolved out of a $115 million federal stimulus award to construct new fiber and connect existing lines across the state. Much of the network is now complete, but at first it remained largely in the dark as anticipated private demand was slow to materialize. As the market begins to heat up, a few different deal structures involving the private sector are becoming clear.

First, lease deals are emerging. The Baltimore County Optical Network connects many of the county's schools and public services. The network is also connected to Harford, Carroll, and Howard counties and Baltimore City. The city of Westminster, Maryland, entered into a deal with Ting. Ting leases the city's fiber in order to offer internet service to the community. The network is actively engaged in pursuing additional lease deals with the private sector to deliver broadband access to unserved areas.

Second, fiber connections are being sold to private developers. In Baltimore City, Caves Valley Partners, a real estate firm, paid to extend the public fiber network to a new development. Boasting the city's fastest network connection, the development is quickly attracting tech companies as tenants. Indeed, high-speed internet has become a business necessity. If private telecom remains complacent in certain markets, private companies like Caves Valley will seek out further business with public networks to deliver the service they need at a reasonable price.

Third, the public sector is offering traditional design-bid-build contracts for network expansion. Anne Arundel County entered into such a contract with Broadstripe to service rural and low-density areas using the public network as a backbone. To fulfill the contract, Broadstripe is responsible for delivering and installing the necessary equipment to build out the fiber network. The contract opportunity was passed over by larger companies.

And fourth, public-private partnerships are enabling fiber roll-out to under- and unserved communities. Leveraging the ICBN, Howard County has partnered with Freedom Broadband to deliver high-speed internet with no data caps to 15,000 residences and businesses. The public-private partnership allows Freedom Broadband to loop into the publicly owned fiber network to then continue to connect local residences and commercial buildings on a private network.

In Maryland, public investment in network infrastructure is complimenting the private sector's objectives and facilitating economic development. High-speed internet that does not discriminate based on income, location, or density is welcomed by residents and business owners alike.

To Light It Up Let's Be Smart About Policy

Dark fiber is a key component for creating a network able to support smart cities and the internet of things, but there are roadblocks to utilization. Even so, the public sector is finding innovative ways to expand fiber networks and light up the dark fiber strands lurking beneath streets and sidewalks.

Continued limitations on the ability of municipal governments to invest in innovative technology, especially an inclusive, ubiquitous fiber-enabled network, will pose problems for future smart cities. Regulation often stymies innovation. This is thought of as one-directional: regulations impose restrictions upon the private sector, limiting incentives and the pathway toward growth. In this case, the effect is in the other direction: regulations are preventing public sectoradoption and innovation.

While the private sector is leading the technical push toward smart cities, the broader public policy goals of improvements in standards of living and economic growth need to be considered. The argument made against public networks is that limiting public sector involvement will protect taxpayers from high costs of building and from mismanagement of the network. Proponents of these restrictions overlook the ability of the public sector to bring in external expertise, however. It is also argued that the public sector entering the market is unfair competition, as government is not profit-motivated. Even though a recent study analyzing municipal fibercash flows found only 2 out of 20 networks to be profitable, the study suggests municipal networks have the potential to indeed be profitable.

Failing to encourage the innovativeness of the public sector will be detrimental to the future of smart cities. For the purpose of unlocking dark fiber, all options should be on the table, including municipal broadband and networks delivered through public-private partnerships. How these networks will evolve over time is difficult to predict. Nonetheless, artificial restrictions on public sector involvement in fiber prevent new models from even being tested, keeping consumers quite literally in the dark.

Is the Internet of Things Sustainable?

Overview: How IoT Technologies Are Used to Combat Environmental Degradation

Sarath Muraleedharan

Sarath Muraleedharan is an IT professional from Kerala, India.

The Internet of Things (IoT) is currently trending with its ever expanding eco-system of digital sensors, appliances and wearable smart devices. Like other sectors, the role of IoT in sustainable development and environment protection will be crucial in the coming years.

Environmental degradation is occurring all over the world. Land degradation, deforestation and desertification pose a growing threat to food security and water availability. Widespread loss of biological diversity is undermining the productive capacity of terrestrial and aquatic ecosystems. This reduces access to essential environmental goods and services, including vital ecological processes such as water purification, nutrient cycling, control of pollution and soil erosion. Environmental degradation exacerbates the frequency and impact of droughts, floods, forest fires and other natural hazards.

Water Management

IoT enables understanding of changes in water quality of a particular reservoir. The connection of different sensors and monitoring systems help in providing the water level and flood warnings as well as foresee other disasters such as earthquakes and potential landslides in prone areas, assisting the civilians and authorities to take drastic action on such issues.

"Role of Internet of Things (IoT) in Sustainable Development," by Sarath Muraleedharan, Ecomena, November 15, 2019. Reprinted by permission.

Agriculture

Smart and adaptive irrigation and agriculture systems in which the soil water content and nutrients are continuously tracked and appropriate actions are taken on the reported deficiency or damage are also gaining huge popularity among the farming communities.

Wildlife

IoT also allow real time detection of animals. In case of any disease outbreaks, it will be useful for control, survey and prevention of such scenarios. For this, the livestock would be fitted with special chips (RFID) and readers would for placed in the designated monitoring spots. Applications like eBird helps the scientists in keeping tracks of birds as well as their habits and migration patterns. Systems that triggers alert on uncontrolled deforestation and potential wildfires can also help the respective authorities to protect and maintain the forests and its inhabitants.

Marine Organisms

Overfishing and over-exploitation of aquatic diversity is endangering high-value species like salmon and cod. ThisFish, an internet tracking network, in association with local bodies help to trace back the fish to the fisherman who caught it and the location through GPS readings and toll data. In this way bad fishing behaviors can be detected and stopped. FishPal provides reports on the type and quantity of fishes caught daily and monthly that can be checked by the fisheries department and also informs suspicious fishing activities.

Buildings

Those who dismissed smart home technology as unrealistic playthings for lazy youngsters are increasingly finding it hard to resist the charms of IoT-powered smart home devices. These devices will become hugely popular in the coming years as they become highly intuitive and innovative, extending to not just home automation comfort but also home security and the safety of your family. That is the kind of home sustainability that will keep the power consumption in check and make optimal use of renewable energy.

Even smart workplaces with Green Design are contributing highly towards energy conservation. With maximum use of daylight, rainwater capture, smart cooling and ventilation systems, solar power etc ensure maximum efficiency in power use and full utilization to renewable sources.

Waste Management

One of the major issues faced in the urban areas is the inefficient waste management. Improper disposal of waste can cause various health hazards and affect the surrounding air and water. The machine-to-machine or machine-to-man (M2M) systems can be established for a much intelligent division and disposal of waste. The trash cans or the dumpsters can have built-in sensors to measure the amount of trash. Once the trash is full, the signal transceiver sends a message to the central command centre via internet or satellite with the GPS location and the IP address.

Use of such Industrial IoT solutions and devices for waste management helps in determining the best time to collect the wastes and figuring out better routes for the collection trucks handling the potential waste build up scenario in cities.

Such smart waste management systems can also help in identifying the different types of waste, such as domestic or commercial, and dividing them based on their degrading ability and processes. This would help in proper disposal for all kind of waste causing less environmental issues and keep track of the ever-growing issue of e-waste management.

Wastewater

SeWatch, a wastewater and sewerage wireless monitoring system, provides a system-wide reporting solution for combined sewer overflow and sanitary sewer overflow discharge or overflow. Water level sensors for sewer system manholes relay information to an application running on a PC or server which alerts on computer screen or via SMS about manhole overflow and spill-over.

A Shining Example

China has come up with a "Sensing China" strategy. It is an environmental protection and overall industrial pollution control system featuring real-time data perception, resource concentration and sharing, system integration as well as effective supervision and decision-making that established to improve the environment and prevent environmental accidents. The specific tasks include intelligent sensors and automatic monitoring devices, wireless monitoring for pollution treatment, water quality data monitoring, air monitoring system, and regional ecological monitoring.

Conclusion

Connected devices promise to be the major drivers of change within the coming few years. With higher demands for this technology from both public and private sector for better energy distribution, accurate business forecasts, the fruits of Green IT and an answer to many of the environment challenges faced by the region, the overall production gains is expected to shoot up. Of course, new technologies, such as Artificial Intelligence, will emerge making IoT more intuitive and user friendly, but largely, manufacturers will have to work harder at securing their connected devices as the risk to data will also increase. Amid all of these trends and predictions, the future ahead is definitely a promising one and certainly worth looking forward to.

How IoT Technologies Can Make Cities Sustainable

Shufan Zhang

Shufan Zhang graduated from the University of Michigan with a degree from the University of Michigan's architecture program.

Internet of Things is a concept of connecting daily objects with an interactive network through wireless communication mediums such as Radio-Frequency Identification (RFID) tags, sensors, and smartphones.[6] IoT has the potential to be applied in many fields, such as industry, transportation, and civic infrastructure.[7] While the different application fields require different IoT frameworks and technology, this article focuses on the "Urban IoT," which establishes an information infrastructure to manage and optimize public services.[8] The application of IoT technology is believed to be an important technological trend in the Smart Cities movement, as mentioned in the APA initiative.[9] It is described as a "building block to realize a unified urban-scale information-communication technology (ICT) platform, thus unleashing the potential of the Smart City vision."[10] The sensor network that detects specific environmental data is a typical application of IoT in sustainable development. Its implementation requires three infrastructural components: sensing, cloud computing, and data. Although the three components are listed from the technological perspective, behind them there is a series of social demands, economic drivers, and governmental requirements.

Sustainability

Like Smart Cities, sustainability is not a new term for urban planning theory and practice. Its definition is highly contentious and debated in planning literature. Because this article aims to

"The Application of the Internet of Things to Enhance Urban Sustainability," by Shufan Zhang, Regents of the University of Michigan, 2017. Reprinted by permission.

provide a background of research for urban planners on the application of the Internet of Things in sustainability fields, the definition of sustainability here also must tie to the urban planning field. Among the various aspects of sustainability, one of the aspects states that sustainability is a mode of development that guarantees a coherent, continuing balance between supply and demand. According to the APA, there are three specific outcomes required for sustainable urban planning:[11]

- A sustainable development should have a plan that ensures equality among all groups.
- The communities built based on sustainable principles should be "resilient, diverse and self-sufficient."
- A sustainable development should contribute to a "healthy" environment, not only from the natural perspective, but also from economic and social perspectives.

From the three outcomes listed above, it is clear that sustainability for urban planning is a concept beyond just the handling of natural resources; rather, sustainability is regarded as a paradigm expected to apply to various aspects of society. In fact, the definition of sustainability still is controversial for its vagueness and inconsistency.[12] Because this article examines the application of IoT technology at an urban scale, which is primarily concerned with environmental sensor networks at this stage, this article chooses the environmental aspect of sustainability as the definitional proof for investigation and arguments.

Role of IoT in Sustainability

IoT is believed to be a significant method among the information-communication technologies involved with the Smart Cities movement, particularly in the domain of sustainable development. Because the application of IoT is deeply embedded in the context of Smart Cities, which serves as a paradigm for the development of IoT technology, planners should be able to draw a link between Smart Cities and the notion of sustainability. Conceptually, the APA

Smart Cities and Sustainability Initiative regards Smart Cities as an extension of sustainability in that Smart Cities seeks to maximize benefits for the most people with minimal costs and impacts, which echoes the very goal of sustainability.[13] In a model that divides Smart Cities into multiple layers, the "green city layer" also indicates the potential that the Smart Cities concept has in improving the environment.[14] An example of this can be found in the Smart Cities Initiative of the European Strategic Energy Technology Plan, which seeks to reduce greenhouse gas emissions by 40 percent by 2020 through Smart City implementations.[15] However, there are also voices contending that the bond between the concept of Smart Cities and ecological sustainability is still weak, in that the Smart City idea is used more for marketing than for infrastructural needs.[16]

Smart Cities, the basis for the application of IoT technology in the urban context, has established its conceptual connection with sustainability. Before exploring the specific ways of evaluating the performance by IoT in urban sustainable development, it is essential to understand the primary position IoT has in the entire process of sustainable development. As introduced before, the application of IoT technology within the field of sustainability is primarily through a sensor network that detects certain data. The data collected by the IoT sensor network would be used to evaluate existing environmental conditions, track performance of certain devices, or optimize future actions in some environmental measurements. All these functions of IoT application are associated with information collection in the preliminary stage of problem solving. This is not to say that IoT technology is at a secondary position in the sustainable development process. Although it appears that IoT technology does not seem to be a "critical" step, the information collected through the sensor network built by IoT technology is of great importance in understanding environmental performance or resource consumption.

[…]

Ownership of Data

Most of the literature on IoT emphasizes the significant meaning of IoT for city administrators in terms of optimized management.[23] However, there arises the issue of the ownership of data retrieved from the sensor network. The administrator-centric mode is a common feature within the Smart Cities movement, neglecting the fact that a great amount of data is related to citizens and users.[24] The absence of public access to data may lead to a difficulty for citizens when perceiving the benefits of a sensor network, leading to an increased difficulty in obtaining funding and public support.

In fact, the process of collecting data from the public domain in the application of sensor networks can have dualistic interpretations in terms of data ownership. On one hand, public participation in this process is a form of citizen science with a great potential of incorporating public efforts within Smart Cities movements.[25]

On the other hand, the monitoring relationship between citizens and environmental data remains vague. Referred to as a scientific method enacted and realized by citizens from non-scientific fields, citizen science is not believed to be a mature mechanism. It is difficult to find the balance between public participation as "raw material" and professional interference as "processing efforts."[26] In the case of IoT sensor networks' purpose to capture environmental data all over the city, the public should have access to the knowledge of what the data collected is used for as an important means of citizen science application. In response to the concern for ownership of data collected from the sensor network, urban planners need to make a stronger effort to build a bridge between professionals and the public in order to incorporate public participation within Smart Cities movements. This is particularly important for projects using data directly from households, such as smart home monitoring and smart grid data tracking.

[…]

Conclusion

The challenges of IoT are often entangled in a complex chain. Therefore, they may need to be resolved together instead of separately. For instance, the span of the sensor network is an essential factor that determines the cost of building such infrastructure, which in turn may impact the public and private sectors' incentive to invest in the project. The issue of security and privacy would also affect the public's willingness to participate, and thus result in a gap between the public and decision makers. In many cases, the challenges cannot be separated and the relationship between factors must be examined in order to untangle and work past the complex series of obstacles present in the implementation process.

To resolve the entangled challenges faced by the IoT network for building a more sustainable city, the mere power of urban planners is not sufficient. As technologies of Smart Cities develop, it will be impossible to realize the framework's potential if any sector is isolated and working in a silo. In the case of Smart Cities, collaboration is particularly important because of the multiple layers of the movement including business, technology, politics, and economics. Urban planners sit at the intersection of these fields, but their impact has been limited to this point. This article suggests that in the application of IoT technology, urban planners would do well to apprehend the importance of understanding and enhancing collaboration among various sectors.

Endnotes

6. Luigi Atzori, Antonio Iera, and Giacomo Morabito. "The Internet of Things: A Survey." *Computer Networks* 54 (15) (2010): 2787-2805.

7. Harald Sundmaeker, Patrick Guillemin, Peter Friess, and Sylvie Woelfflé. 2010. "Vision and Challenges for Realising the Internet of Things." *Cluster of European Research Projects on the Internet of Things*, European Commision.

8. Andrea Zanella, Nicola Bui, Angelo Castellani, Lorenzo Vangelista, and Michele Zorzi. 2014. "Internet of Things for Smart Cities." *IEEE Internet of Things Journal* 1 (1): 22-32.

9. American Planning Association. "Smart Cities and Sustainability Initiative." (2015): 6.

10. Ibid.

11. American Planning Association. *APA Policy Guide for Planning for Sustainability.* https://www.planning.org/policy/guides/ adopted/sustainability.htm

12. Marino Gatto. "Sustainability: Is It a Well Defined Concept?" (1995): 1181-1183.

13. American Planning Association. *APA Policy Guide for Planning for Sustainability.* https://www.planning.org/policy/guides/ adopted/sustainability.html

14. Sotiris Zygiaris. "Smart City Reference Model: Assisting Planners to Conceptualize the Building of Smart City Innovation Ecosystems." *Journal of the Knowledge Economy* 4 (2) (2013): 217-231.

15. Ibid.

16. Anna Kramers, Mattias Höjer, Nina Lövehagen, and Josefin Wangel. "Smart Sustainable Cities–Exploring ICT Solutions for Reduced Energy Use in Cities." *Environmental Modelling & Software* 56 (2014): 52-62.

23. American Planning Association. *APA Policy Guide for Planning for Sustainability.* https://www.planning.org/policy/guides/ adopted/sustainability.html

24. Adam Greenfield. *Against the Smart City: A Pamphlet.* Do Projects 2013.

25. Janis L. Dickinson, Jennifer Shirk, David Bonter, Rick Bonney, Rhiannon L. Crain, Jason Martin, Tina Phillips, and Karen Purcell. "The Current State of Citizen Science as a Tool for Ecological Research and Public Engagement." *Frontiers in Ecology and the Environment* 10 (6) (2012): 291-297.

26. Karin Bäckstrand. "Civic Science for Sustainability: Reframing the Role of Experts, Policy-Makers and Citizens in Environmental Governance." *Global Environmental Politics* 3 (4) (2003): 24-41.

How IoT Will Revolutionize Waste Management

Neil Sequeira

Neil Sequeira is a writer whose work has appeared in publications such as Forbes *and IoT for All*

O ur attention has been increasingly brought to the need to manage, reduce, recycle and reuse the mountains of waste generated in cities every day. While this is by no means an easy task, technology has stepped in to help us make everyday city management operations more sustainable. As IoT's impact on the waste management industry increases, the future of recycling looks promising. IoT applications in waste management are effectively improving municipal operations. Predefined routes and outdated methods of waste collection are increasingly being replaced with sensor-enabled bins and sophisticated waste management applications.

Using IoT Data to Recycle Products

The success of any IoT-enabled application lies in the collection of a vast amount of data, often in real-time, and the distillation of those data into insights on which users can take action. As sensor technology advances, a whole array of everyday objects are being connected to the internet (and to each other) to exchange information interactively.

The most common IoT application in waste management operations currently is the automated route optimization of garbage pickup trucks. These trucks generally follow a specific route every day to collect trash. For those sanitation departments that have yet to harness IoT connectivity, the drivers generally don't know

"IoT Applications in Waste Management," by Neil Sequeira, IoT for All, January 29, 2020. Reprinted by permission.

how full a trash bin is before they encounter it. That results in a lot of wasted time, fuel, and therefore money.

IoT applications in waste management are improving this scenario by giving sanitation workers insight into the actual fill level of various disposal units, whose loads can vary by the day, the week, and the season.

Sensor-enabled and internet-connected garbage bins can collect information on fill level, temperature, location, or whatever data types the sensors gather and the sanitation department finds useful. With a user interface revealing the locations and fill levels of all bins, waste collectors can get an automated route planned for them that has prioritized areas in urgent need of cleanup and avoided disposal units that still have room.

Not only are these bins optimizing fleet logistics operations and reducing fuel consumption, but they're also recording the number of times they're emptied and how fast they fill up. Such data, when combined with statistics from other smart city systems, can facilitate more insightful, multi-pronged actions, such as planning the better distribution of garbage bins, zeroing on problems (e.g. incorrect disposal practices), or reducing waste going to the landfill.

Sanitation departments are beginning to unlock new value by leveraging IoT applications in waste management. For example, ISB Global is using IoT-powered applications to manage waste more effectively. Using sensors installed on each bin, cloud-based data collection and synthesis, and a user interface/smart app, ISB has created a network of connected devices for effective waste management. Their systems also capture data such as weight, volume, costs, truck number, and feed all the information back which can further automate billing and invoicing operations. This is but one example of a company pushing the envelope with IoT application in waste management. More innovation and standardization are needed.

Technology Can Help Where Humans Struggle

The next step for "digital bins" lies in automating the categorization of waste content, a task at which most people make mistakes. Polish company Bin-e has come up with "Smart Waste Bins" capable of identifying and sorting waste into up to four categories: glass, paper, plastic, and metal.

The Bins then compress the waste and notify sanitation workers of fill levels for each waste category. Intelligent categorization and segregation is an upcoming trend. It's still being refined for larger-scale deployments.

Bringing Citizens to the Forefront

Smart Bins like those above have the potential to raise stakeholders' awareness of the power of IoT applications in waste management by providing them with visibility into their daily waste footprint. By integrating inputs from hardware units (sensors) into software applications, we can allow sanitation departments better to analyze waste patterns and optimize routes while also allowing everyday citizens to manage their consumption and waste habits more sustainability.

Even Smart Packaging with digital tags (QR codes, Barcodes, Datamatrix codes, RFID & NFC tags) can play a part in ensuring people recycle and dispose of waste responsibly. Those confused can rapidly pull up instructions on how to dispose of a particular item in an interactive format, by a simple scan of the digital tags with their smartphones.

But what about e-waste items such as large batteries or electronics? Electronics contain platinum, gold, silver, lithium, and palladium as well as other raw materials such as iron, copper, and aluminum—all valuable resources that can be recycled and reused.

With the breakneck pace at which electronics are penetrating every aspect of our world, the amount of e-waste we generate is likely only to climb. This opens up a whole new set of opportunities for businesses to use digital twins of sanitation systems to recycle e-waste for precious and finite resources.

The Future of IoT Applications in Waste Management

The ultimate goal of IoT applications in waste management is producing leaner operations and delivering higher quality services to citizens. A growing collection of interlinked autonomous systems are managing everyday urban operations and improving both citizen experiences and our carbon footprint. Ultimately, however, we need deeper coordination between public sectors—through a mix of regulation and incentives—and private sectors—through a willingness to engage with regional, state, and federal agencies to use IoT applications in waste management to build a better and more sustainable future.

"Smart Farming" Will Sustainably Feed the World

Savaram Ravindra

Savaram Ravindra is a content writer at a website called Mindmajix.

The global population is predicted to touch 9.6 billion by 2050—this poses a big problem for the agriculture industry. Despite combating challenges like extreme weather conditions, rising climate change, and farming's environmental impact, the demand for more food has to be met. To meet these increasing needs, agriculture has to turn to new technology. New smart farming applications based on IoT technologies will enable the agriculture industry to reduce waste and enhance productivity from optimizing fertilizer use to increasing the efficiency of farm vehicles' routes.

So, what is smart farming? Smart farming is a capital-intensive and hi-tech system of growing food cleanly and sustainable for the masses. It is the application of modern ICT (Information and Communication Technologies) into agriculture.

In IoT-based smart farming, a system is built for monitoring the crop field with the help of sensors (light, humidity, temperature, soil moisture, etc.) and automating the irrigation system. The farmers can monitor the field conditions from anywhere. IoT-based smart farming is highly efficient when compared with the conventional approach.

The applications of IoT-based smart farming not only target conventional, large farming operations, but could also be new levers to uplift other growing or common trends in agricultural like organic farming, family farming (complex or small spaces, particular cattle and/or cultures, preservation of particular or high-quality varieties, etc.), and enhance highly transparent farming.

"IoT Applications in Agriculture," Savaram Ravindra, IoT for All, January 29, 2020. Reprinted by permission.

In terms of environmental issues, IoT-based smart farming can provide great benefits including more efficient water usage, or optimization of inputs and treatments. Now, let's discuss the major applications of IoT-based smart farming that are revolutionizing agriculture.

Applications of IoT in Agriculture

Precision Farming

Also known as precision agriculture, precision farming can be thought of as anything that makes farming practice more controlled and accurate when it comes to raising livestock and growing crops. In this approach of farm management, a key component is the use of IT and various items like sensors, control systems, robotics, autonomous vehicles, automated hardware, variable rate technology, and so on.

The adoption of access to high-speed internet, mobile devices, and reliable, low-cost satellites (for imagery and positioning) by the manufacturer are a few key technologies characterizing the precision agriculture trend.

Precision agriculture is one of the most famous applications of IoT in the agricultural sector and numerous organizations are leveraging this technique around the world. CropMetrics is a precision agriculture organization focused on ultra-modern agronomic solutions while specializing in the management of precision irrigation.

The products and services of CropMetrics include VRI optimization, soil moisture probes, virtual optimizer PRO, and so on. VRI (Variable Rate Irrigation) optimization maximizes profitability on irrigated crop fields with topography or soil variability, improve yields, and increases water use efficiency.

The soil moisture probe technology provides complete in-season local agronomy support, and recommendations to optimize water use efficiency. The virtual optimizer PRO combines various technologies for water management into one central, cloud-based, and powerful location designed for consultants and growers to take advantage of the benefits in precision irrigation via a simplified interface.

Agricultural Drones

Technology has changed over time and agricultural drones are a very good example of this. Today, agriculture is one of the major industries to incorporate drones. Drones are being used in agriculture in order to enhance various agricultural practices. The ways ground-based and aerial-based drones are being used in agriculture are crop health assessment, irrigation, crop monitoring, crop spraying, planting, and soil and field analysis.

The major benefits of using drones include crop health imaging, integrated GIS mapping, ease of use, saves time, and the potential to increase yields. With strategy and planning based on real-time data collection and processing, drone technology will give a high-tech makeover to the agriculture industry.

PrecisionHawk is an organization that uses drones for gathering valuable data via a series of sensors that are used for imaging, mapping, and surveying of agricultural land. These drones perform in-flight monitoring and observations. The farmers enter the details of what field to survey and select an altitude or ground resolution.

From the drone data, we can draw insights regarding plant health indices, plant counting and yield prediction, plant height measurement, canopy cover mapping, field water ponding mapping, scouting reports, stockpile measuring, chlorophyll measurement, nitrogen content in wheat, drainage mapping, weed pressure mapping, and so on.

The drone collects multispectral, thermal, and visual imagery during the flight and then lands in the same location it took off.

Livestock Monitoring

Large farm owners can utilize wireless IoT applications to collect data regarding the location, well-being, and health of their cattle. This information helps them in identifying animals that are sick so they can be separated from the herd, thereby preventing the spread of disease. It also lowers labor costs as ranchers can locate their cattle with the help of IoT based sensors.

JMB North America is an organization that offers cow monitoring solutions to cattle producers. One of the solutions helps the cattle owners observe cows that are pregnant and about to give birth. From the heifer, a sensor powered by a battery is expelled when its water breaks. This sends information to the herd manager or the rancher. In the time that is spent with heifers that are giving birth, the sensor enables farmers to be more focused.

Smart Greenhouses

Greenhouse farming is a methodology that helps in enhancing the yield of vegetables, fruits, crops, etc. Greenhouses control the environmental parameters through manual intervention or a proportional control mechanism. As manual intervention results in production loss, energy loss, and labor costs, these methods are less effective. A smart greenhouse can be designed with the help of IoT; this design intelligently monitors as well as controls the climate, eliminating the need for manual intervention.

For controlling the environment in a smart greenhouse, different sensors that measure the environmental parameters according to the plant requirement are used. We can create a cloud server for remotely accessing the system when it is connected using IoT.

This eliminates the need for constant manual monitoring. Inside the greenhouse, the cloud server also enables data processing and applies a control action. This design provides cost-effective and optimal solutions for farmers with minimal manual intervention.

Illuminum Greenhouses is a drip installation and Agri-Tech greenhouse organization and uses new modern technologies for providing services. It builds modern and affordable greenhouses by using solar-powered IoT sensors. With these sensors, the greenhouse state and water consumption can be monitored via SMS alerts to the farmer with an online portal. Automatic Irrigation is carried out in these greenhouses.

The IoT sensors in the greenhouse provide information on the light levels, pressure, humidity, and temperature. These sensors can control the actuators automatically to open a window, turn on lights, control a heater, turn on a mister or turn on a fan, all controlled through a WiFi signal.

Conclusion

Thus, the IoT agricultural applications are making it possible for ranchers and farmers to collect meaningful data. Large landowners and small farmers must understand the potential of IoT market for agriculture by installing smart technologies to increase competitiveness and sustainability in their productions. With the population growing rapidly, the demand can be successfully met if the ranchers, as well as small farmers, implement agricultural IoT solutions in a prosperous manner.

The Internet of Food Will Change How We Eat

Nicholas M. Holden, Eoin P. White, Matthew C. Lange, and Thomas L. Oldfield

Nicholas M. Holden is a professor at the University College Dublin's School of Biosystems and Food Engineering. Eoin P. White is an analyst at CDP Worldwide, a British environmental impact firm. Matthew C. Lange is a professor in the Food Science Technology Department at the University of California Davis. Thomas L. Oldfield studied at the UCD School of Biosystems and Food Engineering in Ireland.

The food we eat today is unsustainable for two reasons: the food system causes unacceptable environmental impacts and it is depleting non-renewable resources. Our food can be regarded as "fossil food" because its production relies on fossil fuel, non-renewable mineral resources, depletion of groundwater reserves and excessive soil loss. The idea of sustainable food systems is at the heart of global efforts to manage and regulate human food supply. The sustainable development goals focus on a number of critical global issues, but Goal 2 ("end hunger, achieve food security and improved nutrition and promote sustainable agriculture"), Goal 12 ("ensure sustainable consumption and production patterns") and Goal 13 ("take urgent action to combat climate change and its impacts") are intimately related to the need to transition global food systems from fossil to sustainable. To understand how to meet the challenge presented by these goals, it is necessary to consider what is meant by "sustainable" in the context of a food system. In 1989, the Food and Agriculture Organisation (FAO) council defined sustainable development as "the management and conservation of the natural resource base, and the orientation of technological and institutional

Holden, N. M., White, E. P., Lange, M. C., et al. "Review of the Sustainability of Food Systems and Transition Using the Internet of Food." *npj Sci Food* 2, 18 (2018). https://doi.org/10.1038/s41538-018-0027-3. Licensed under CC-BY 4.0 International.

change in such a manner as to ensure the attainment and continued satisfaction of human needs for present and future generations. Such sustainable development (in the agriculture, forestry and fisheries sectors) conserves land, water, plant and animal genetic resources, is environmentally non-degrading, technically appropriate, economically viable and socially acceptable." The important ideas in this definition are working within the planetary boundary ("the natural resource base"), having a future-proof system ("continued satisfaction," "present and future generations"), limiting impacts to those manageable by the buffering capacity of the planet ("environmentally non-degrading"), considering the financial needs of business stakeholders ("economically viable") and compatible with local needs and customs ("socially acceptable").

Five principles have been identified to support a common vision for sustainable agriculture and food. These are: (1) resource efficiency; (2) action to conserve, protect and enhance natural resources; (3) rural livelihood protection and social well-being; (4) enhanced resilience of people, communities and ecosystems; and (5) responsible governance. The aim of this paper is to outline the case for why food systems are not sustainable and to define the case for using technology, specifically internet technologies (hardware and software combined to make the "Internet of Food") to enable the transition of the food system from fossil to sustainable. Increasing population, increasing consumption, a billion malnourished people and agriculture that is concurrently degrading land, water, biodiversity and climate on a global scale combine to indicate that the fossil food systems we currently rely on are not fit-for-purpose. It is suggested that halting agricultural expansion, closing yield gaps, increasing efficiency, changing diets and reducing waste could lead to a doubling of food production with reduced environmental impacts of agriculture. To achieve these changes, it is going to be necessary to harness internet technology, in the form of an "Internet of Food," which offers the chance to use global resources more efficiently, to stimulate rural livelihoods, to develop systems for resilience and to facilitate responsible governance by means of computation, communication, education and trade without limits of knowledge and access.

The concept of "Internet of Food" first appeared in peer-reviewed literature in 2011 (based on a search of scopus.com using "Internet of Food" as the search term). It was described by the idea of food items having an "IP identify," which raised the question of how this might influence our eating habits. Their focus was very much on how the technology could influence food choices and predicted that by 2020 it would be possible to monitor and control food objects remotely through the Internet. It is this technological control of the food system that has real potential to help societal stakeholders (consumers, retailers, processors, producers, shareholders, landowners, indigenous peoples and so on) to engage in the transition of our food system from being fossil to sustainable. The ubiquitous physical tagging and sensing of mass and energy flow in the food system linked to a formal semantic web will allow computation over the whole system to answer questions such as: What was the resource depletion of this product? What is the social impact of eating this product? What food safety procedures have been employed for this product? What and where has wealth been created by the value chain of this product? When these questions can be answered for specific instances of food product types and predicted for new products, then it will be possible to determine whether a specific food system is sustainable or not. The stakeholders demanding answers to these questions are likely to be governance and policy makers and consumers. When these questions can be answered, it will be possible to plan how to manage the evolution of the fundamental life support system (food) from fossil to sustainable in order to support a growing global population.

[...]

Internet of Food: An Enabling Technology for the Transition from Fossil to Sustainable

The deployment of sensor networks in the food system have historically been stage-specific and typically designed for monitoring and decision-making at a specific site and time, despite the potential for system integration having been recognised more than a decade ago. Many sensors have been developed that could be used for the food chain, for example, for soil monitoring, for precision agriculture purposes, for post-harvest storage monitoring, for process control, for retail logistics monitoring and in some cases for domestic use. A key requirement to create an "Internet of Food" will be to make the data from these sensors interoperable and to be able to compute across the data set they create. A notable limitation is lack of integration caused by the current mix of open and closed data, communications, hardware standards and a lack of willingness to share data between stakeholders. It has been noted that an "…ontology-driven architecture for developing hybrid systems [that] consists of various entities including software components, hardware components (sensors, actuators and controllers), datastores (knowledge base, raw data, metadata), biological elements (plants[or animals]) and environmental context…" would permit the development of precision agriculture applications, and by logical extension this is required to utilise information across the whole food system (i.e. the Internet of Food). The proposal here is that the "hybrid-system" needs to be extended to cover the whole food system, thus permitting production, process, logistics, retail, purchasing, consumption, nutrition and health outcomes to be integrated through information and computation. Where it is not possible to integrate data of the whole system that delivers a product, it will be very difficult to use Internet of Food for best advantage because its strength is determined by the data available.

A critical requirement will be the development of related ontologies. An ontology is the formal naming of concepts (e.g. types, properties, inter-relationships) within a domain and it is used to describe or infer properties of that domain. In order to be able to draw upon a range of data sources (sensors) and databases (knowledge silos), it is necessary to label data with unique identifiers that permit computers to reason with or compute over those data sets. This is where the real value of Internet of Things, and more specifically Internet of Food lies. To achieve the paradigm shift from fossil food to sustainable food systems, such a shift is needed, facilitated by the ability to reason with such data. As noted, an ontology-driven architecture is needed to enable the "Internet of Food." Ecologists have recognised the importance of big data in ecological research in order to address major scientific and societal issues, and to answer the major question facing food (how to achieve a sustainable food system?), an agreed vocabulary and language structure (ontology) is needed. To take simple examples, the word "buttermilk" originally referred to liquid left after churning butter is now also used to describe a fermented or cultured milk drink, so until the language describing these two concepts is standardised it is not possible to compute from diverse data sets within the domain of dairy processing, never mind across domains, where words such as slurry, matrix and texture all mean very different things depending on context. A noted rapid growth of Internet of Things requires standardisation to lower the entry barriers for the new services, to improve interoperability of systems and to allow better services performance. They noted that this is particularly important for security, communication and identification where interoperability, and particularly semantic interoperability, will be critical. It has been recognised that a proliferation of ad hoc coded data systems will be an impediment to developing data-centric systems that can transform farming, so sharing of data, agreement of standards and stakeholder cooperation will be required to achieve food systems transformation.

Food ontologies can be used with the specific aim of identifying gaps and for purposes beyond the initial, relatively simple applications, such as recognising foods, with a contextual focus on diet, food selection, health and wellbeing being possible, which is a critical component of a sustainable food system, and just as important are the social, economic and environmental impacts and benefits. There are untold opportunities to develop specific services targeted in these areas as well as the potential for integration, with tools such as life cycle sustainability assessment to evaluate the true sustainability of specific food products, meal combinations, whole diets and food systems. These ideas have been evaluated in the context of mining US EPA data for assessing chemical manufacturing, which identified that automating data access was a challenge because the data are incompatible with semantic queries. Data need to be described using ontologies to relate those data that need to be linked and to introduce LCA concepts to the descriptions. A framework for integrating "big data" with LCA has been suggested and it was also noted that development of semantic web standards for ecological data have greatly enhanced interoperability in that domain. The same is required for the food system. It has been suggested that when food (and water) domain descriptors have been developed, this will enable "IT support [for] improved production, distribution and sales of foodstuffs [and water]," but the development of the domain models for the food chain is perhaps not a task for commerce or industry, rather for public, international research.

The opportunities that will be created by the Internet of Food are immense. One important shift will be from a descriptive, inferential approach to analysing food systems to a "big data" approach. "Big data" can be characterised in terms of volume (data sets too large for conventional database management), velocity (acquiring, understanding and interpreting data in real time) and variety (the vast array of sources and types of data beyond the conventional rows and columns of numbers describing transactions). Examples have already emerged where "big data" has been used to provide data useful for LCA including agricultural resource survey and resource use and emissions associated with US electric power generation. It is worth pointing out that much of the data relied on for LCA studies is drawn from commonly used databases (e.g. EcoInvent, ELCD, NREL) and are reliant on "small data" and limited observations, which has resulted in reported error (multiple orders of magnitude), while "big data" offers a means to answering questions about environmental impact or food safety that simply cannot be contemplated in the context of controlled experiments.

Authors have considered "big data" and "internet of things" in the context of specific parts of the food chain. For example, "big data" in "smart farming" (i.e. the production stage of the food system) is now being used to make predictive insights about farm operations, to support operational decisions, to redesign business processes and to change business models. To leverage this value at the farm level required extension along the food chain beyond the farm, but two scenarios are emerging: closed proprietary systems and open collaborative systems, such as Food Industry Intelligence Network, Food Innovation Network and European Institute of Innovation & Technology (EIT) Food. Priority should be given to development of data and applications infrastructure and at the same time to organisational issues concerning governance and business models for data sharing. In the context of circular economy (i.e. the end of life, non-consumed part of the food system), it was found that, despite the concept of circular economy being discussed for decades, it has not become an adopted business model. An analysis of literature from 2006 to 2015 found only 70 publications at the intersection of circular economy and "big data"/"internet of things," but nearly half (34) had been published in 2015. It was suggested that technology encompassed by "big data" and "internet of things" is what is needed to enable such change, which is the same argument being put forward here for the Internet of Food in the context of sustainable food systems. Two implications of relevance for the Internet of Food are: there is a gap between scientific research and corporate initiatives, which needs to be closed, and the search of literature was limited by the keywords available, and more specifically the lack of structured taxonomy to describe the circular economy. It is reasonable to conclude that if these ideas are relevant to one small component of the Internet of Food, then they are probably relevant to the concept as a whole.

These two recent reviews highlight the importance of developing the Internet of Food as a precompetitive platform on which business models can be built, much like the internet as we currently know it, and to achieve this we need to define agreed vocabularies and ontologies to be able to reason and compute across the vast amounts of data that are and will be available in the future. The ability to compute over large amounts of data will change the way the food system is analysed and understood. Biological scientists have noted how important data curation is, because as curated data become available the way science is conducted changes. A key requirement of data curation is the connection of data from different sources in a human- and machine-comprehensible way. Another key change is the processing of multiple sources of complex data ("big data") using inference programs. While this might lead to new ways of conducting experimental (hypothesis driven) research, it is also unlocking the door to data-driven research, i.e. extracting new knowledge and understanding from data without experimentation or preconceived ideas, and providing new management approaches based on information and better decision-making capabilities.

The Internet of Food offers substantial opportunities for understanding the limits and constraints to sustainable food systems and thus supporting decisions about the transition from fossil to sustainable food. It is essential that all stakeholders engage with the development of Internet of Food to ensure harmonious development of a technology that can be used for both pre-competitive applications and commercial exploitation, if it is to be fully developed over the coming 5–10 years. In addition to the technical issues highlighted here, there are considerations of data ownership, privacy, ethical use of data, market control and other application domains (e.g. food safety, traceability, personal nutrition, security, fraud and policy) that need to be developed with stakeholder contributions alongside the technical advances considered here.

Conclusions

In order to transition to a sustainable food system, we need specific technology infrastructure to allow high-quality data to be collected about the food system that will permit the best possible decision-making. Key requirements are: standard vocabularies and ontologies to allow integration of data sets across the internet; proliferation of low cost sensing to allow orders of magnitude change in the supply of empirical observation data into LCA models; and new analytical methods to collate, curate, analyse and utilise data across the whole food production system. We need an Internet of Food to monitor conditions and analyse data to derive knowledge that can be combined with the means to implement control of the system to enable a step change in how we think about food systems. This technology will give us the chance to transition from fossil food to sustainable food systems.

The Environmental Impact of the Internet of Things

Laura-Diana Radu

Laura-Diana Radu is a graduate of Alexandru Ioan Cuza University, a public university in Romania.

The Internet of Things (IoT) is an extension of the Internet and consists of a very large number of computing devices communicating with each other to perform various tasks. The first use of the concept was in 1998, by Kevin Ashton. He said that: "The Internet of Things has the potential to change the world, just as the Internet did. Maybe even more so." (Ashton, 2009) The IoT has seen a steady growth in last decades due to the evolution of information and communication technologies (ICT). The World Wide Web has evolved rapidly from Web 1.0 to Web 2.0 and Web 3.0. However, the last generation has been one of transition to Web 4.0, which is IoT. Web 4.0 is open and intelligent and is about the ultra-intelligent electronic agent. (Fowler & Rodd, 2016) According to Perera et al. (2013), the IoT has not revolutionized people's lives or the field of computing; it is just another step in the evolution of the Internet. However, IoT comes with a wide variety of challenges. It is a world full of smart objects that promises to improve business processes and human lives, but it brings with it serious threats that must be solved and technical challenges that must be overcome. (Whitmore et al., 2015) Most of these challenges are in the field of data security and confidentiality. (Georgescu & Popescul, 2016) According to Miorandi et al. (2012), from a conceptual point of view, the IoT is based on three pillars, related to the ability of smart objects to: (i) be identifiable (anything identifies itself), (ii) to communicate (anything communicates) and (iii) to interact (anything interacts)—either among themselves, building networks of interconnected objects, or with end-users or other entities in the network. Unlike the traditional Internet, where the main producers and consumers of data and information are people, in the IoT objects generate and use the largest amount of data and information. These objects are highly varied and have different complexities. Some are small devices with limited computation capabilities, such as Radio Frequency Identification tags (RFIDs); others are very complex, such as smartphones, smart appliances and smart vehicles. Each relevant component has the potential to become proactive and self-managing. In IoT, objects are able to understand the objects in the physical world and to respond promptly to events outside of themselves.

The aim of this paper is to identify the main research challenges for the positive and negative influence of the IoT on the environment. The rest of this paper is organized as follows. Section 2 reviews the IoT, both present and future. In Section 3, the problem statement is presented. The positive and negative effects of the IoT's development and its effect on the environment are presented in Section 4. Finally, Section 5 concludes the study.

Related Work

The IoT is the next step in the evolution of the Internet. People are excited about the opportunities and changes brought about by these technologies, such as smart cities, smart power grids, smart wearables, smart supply chain, etc. The development of IoT has been favoured by technological advances and by a reduction in the cost of production and the use of ICT. Its implementation involves billions of online objects that communicate and change their status according to users' preferences and environmental changes. Like any complex and growing technology, the IoT has been defined by different authors in many different ways depending on the component under consideration. Atzori et al. (2010) identified three different visions for the IoT: "Internet oriented" (middleware), "things oriented" (sensors) and "semantic oriented" (knowledge). Different definitions of the IoT, and the main technologies, concepts and standards according to these paradigms, are presented in Table 1.

Beyond these different approaches, one of the most popular definitions is that given by Vermesan et al. (2011), who stated that the IoT "allows people and things to be connected Anytime, Anyplace, with Anything and Anyone, ideally using Any path/ network and Any service."

The IoT requires massive investment and significant changes in infrastructure, communications, interfaces, protocols and standards. (Li et al., 2015) At present, the concept is an important subject of political and economic debate, because it is expected to stimulate new business opportunities in the field of ICT and in other industries. (Ardito et al., 2017) The increase in the number of Internet connected devices supports these concerns. According to Rayn and Watson (2017), at present only 0.6% of objects have the potential to be part of the IoT, but the number of devices could be as high as 50 billion by 2020, far greater than the number of human users. Another study made by Gartner points out that the consumer segment is the largest user of connected things.

An important question is: how environmental-friendly will these devices be? The increasing number of devices able to communicate with each other to perform different tasks has both positive and negative effects. For the natural environment, the most important issues are increasing the volume of e-waste, energy consumption and CO_2 emissions. As a result, features like the robustness of devices and energy efficiency are very important for minimizing these influences. On the other side of positive influences, devices for monitoring airborne quality, radiation, water quality, hazardous airborne chemicals and many other environmental indicators bring significant benefits in terms of quality of life. They could be an important source of information for finding sustainable solutions to environmental issues.

TABLE 1. IoT PARADIGMS		
PARADIGM	DEFINITION	TECHNOLOGIES, CONCEPTS AND STANDARDS
Internet oriented	"IoT will be deployed by means of a sort of simplification of the current IP to adapt it to any object and make those objects addressable and reachable from any location." (Atzori et al., 2010)	IP for smart objects (IPSO), WoT, Internet Ø
Things oriented	"Things" are "active participants in business, information and social processes where they are enabled to interact and communicate among themselves and with the environment by exchanging data and information 'sensed' about the environment, while reacting autonomously to the 'real/physical world' events and influencing it by running processes that trigger actions and create services with or without direct human intervention." (Sundmaeker et al., 2010, p. 43)	RFID, UID, NFC, WSN, Spimes, Smart Items
Semantic oriented	"The Semantic Sensor (&Actuator) Web is an extension of the current Web/Internet in which information is given well-defined meaning, better enabling objects, devices and people to work in co-operation and to also enable autonomous interactions between devices and/or objects." (Barnaghi, 2014)	Semantic Technologies, Reasoning over dynamic data, SEE

Problem Statement

All people have a role in reducing the negative impact on the environment in both their personal and professional lives. To fulfil this role, they need to be informed and to have a favourable legal framework provided by regulatory institutions. For this reason, in economically and socially stable countries, the level of interest in environmental protection and citizens' initiatives in this direction are more representative. Neuroscientists have shown that people are addicted to information. Panksepp (2004) mentions that our brain contains a seeking system that promotes the spontaneous capacity to explore or investigate information about our world. (Watson et al., 2011) IoT has all of the features needed to meet this constant need for information and, at the same time, performs certain repetitive activities which therefore leave more time for innovation and creativity. However, the environmental impact of IoT has not received the same level of attention as its impact on social life and manufacturing.

Green in IoT vs. Green by IoT

The IoT has brought with it increasing opportunities and challenges for environmental protection. Similar to the relationship between the environment and ICT, the IoT can have both first and second order effects on the environment. (Berkhout & Hertin, 2001, p. 2) A first order effect is the negative impact of ICT production, use and disposal. This effect refers to the physical existence of ICT and the processes it involves. These technologies generate CO_2 emissions, e-waste and the use of harmful substances and non-renewable resources across their entire life cycle. Second order effects are related to the benefits of using ICT to improve the ecologically sustainable development of businesses and society. The contribution of the IoT to environmental protection can be bi-directional: the design and development of energy-efficient IoT devices from recyclable and biodegradable materials and the use of IoT devices to monitor the environment and prevent its degradation. However, the IoT is first and foremost ICT, and ICT has some negative influences on the environment. Nevertheless, by using them in various fields of activity, it helps to reduce the negative effects of human activities on the environment. For example, in supply chains, RFID tags contribute to reducing CO_2 emissions by optimizing flows of perishable goods, ensuring a constant temperature for storing them, tracking the recycling of plastic used by cars, improving waste management, etc. Environmental sensors are used to measure air quality, water quality and radiation level, and to detect the presence of hazardous substances in places in which they would present danger to people or to which they do not have access. The ability to protect the environment must accompany the whole life cycle of IoT technologies through green design, green production, green utilization, and finally, green disposal/recycling so as to have no or very little impact on the environment. (Sathyamoorthy et al., 2015; Zhu et al., 2015)

The most important components and technologies of green IoT are presented in this section. We have identified two perspectives of the relationship of green IoT with the environment, similar to those given by Calero and Piattini (2015) to green ICT projects:

- Green by IoT are initiatives to reduce the environmental impact of operations using the IoT.
- Green in IoT are initiatives to reduce the environmental impact of the IoT.
- A RIFD tag is a very small microchip with a unique identifier that can be attached to objects, animals or people and can receive and send signals. They use radio waves to exchange information, which is read using RFID readers located at different distances depending on the tag type and the device. In Table 2, the ways in which this technology can support environmental protection are presented.

Wireless sensor networks (WSN) are spatially distributed autonomous sensors, which communicate with each other to monitor physical or environmental conditions. (Lee & Lee, 2015) The IoT cannot exist without sensor networks because they provide most of the hardware infrastructure support by providing access to sensors and actuators. (Perera et al., 2014) In Table 3, the ways in which WSN can support environmental protection are presented.

Near Field Communication (NFC) is "a radio device, on a frequency of 13.56 MHz, which can establish the communication between two objects which are in an area of up to 20 cm." (Popescul & Georgescu, 2013) Table 4 presents how NFC supports environmental protection.

TABLE 2. GREEN BY RFID VS. GREEN IN RFID	
GREEN BY RFID	GREEN IN RFID
Wildlife monitoring to collect environmental data, track badgers and deliver this information to geologists (Dyo et al., 2009); Waste management: automatic waste sorting into recyclable materials, restricting the access of unauthorized persons to the waste bins and monitoring the volume of waste produced by each person, etc.; Monitoring nature (e.g., trees, animals) and environmental conservations; Predicting natural disasters (e.g., volcanic eruptions).	Minimize tags to reduce the amount of non-degradable resources that they contain; Using biodegradable materials for tags; Developing and using algorithms and protocols to reduce per-tag energy consumption (Qiao et al., 2011), the number of colliding responses from tags (Namboodiri & Gao, 2007) and adjusting transmission power levels dynamically (Zhu, 2015), etc.

TABLE 3. GREEN BY WSN VS. GREEN IN WSN	
GREEN BY WSN	GREEN IN WSN
Integration of the WSN with energy harvesters; Natural environment monitoring and risk identification (floods, tsunami, air pollution, gas, etc.); Energy savings by switching sensors to low-power operation mode when not in use; Traffic monitoring; Natural resource management (e.g., water, light) necessary in agriculture.	Energy monitoring in smart buildings; Reduction of the volume of data by technics, like network coding, compression, aggregation, etc.; Implementing energy-efficient routing protocols.

TABLE 4. GREEN BY NFC VS. GREEN IN NFC	
GREEN BY NFC	GREEN IN NFC
Optimizing the use of resources according to the presence or absence of people in a particular place (e.g., home, office, parking garage, etc.); Reducing the amount of paper by using NFC technologies to distribute information to potential consumers; Reducing the number of cards by replacing them with apps available on your smartphone.	Using recycled materials for NFC tags; Minimizing energy consumption for active NFC.

Machine-to-machine (M2M) describes "the technologies that enable computers, embedded processors, smart sensors, actuators and mobile devices to communicate with one another, take measurements and make decisions—often without human intervention." (Watson et al., 2004) Table 5 presents how M2M supports environmental protection.

Supervisory control and data acquisition (SCADA) is "a computer-based control system which are used to monitor and control physical processes." (Tsang, 2010) In Table 6, the ways in which this technology contributes to reducing negative impacts on the environment are presented.

Cloud computing is "a model for enabling ubiquitous, convenient, on-demand network access to a shared pool of configurable computing resources (…) that can be rapidly provisioned and released with minimal management effort or service provider interaction." (Mell & Grace, 2009) Table 7 presents how cloud computing supports environmental protection.

TABLE 5. GREEN BY M2M VS. GREEN IN M2M	
GREEN BY M2M	**GREEN IN M2M**
Monitoring energy consumption and gas/oil production;	Harvesting the energy capabilities of the environment;
Smart Grid Monitoring in industries;	Using an efficient nodes schedule and switching to sleep mode when they are not in use;
Smart meters for Home Energy Management Systems (Chen, 2011);	Using distributed computing techniques and developing algorithms for efficient transmission protocols.
Monitoring machine health in industry;	
Monitoring air quality and water treatment and supply;	
Traffic monitoring.	

TABLE 6. GREEN BY SCADA VS. GREEN IN SCADA	
GREEN BY SCADA	GREEN IN SCADA
Optimizing resources consumed, e.g., energy, water, etc., in all production processes;	Using recyclable materials for programmable logic controllers (PLCs) or remote terminal units (RTUs);
Managing information on water resources in the case of floods and cleaning up after them;	Developing and using green software SCADA;
Managing the water reserves necessary for plants in case of drought;	Using the most energy-efficient hardware.
Environmental monitoring under extreme temperatures;	
Monitoring air quality, sound intensity and radiation levels.	

TABLE 7. GREEN BY CLOUD COMPUTING VS. GREEN IN CLOUD COMPUTING	
GREEN BY CLOUD COMPUTING	GREEN IN CLOUD COMPUTING
Using clean energy in data centres;	Provides the hardware and software resources necessary for storing, processing and communicating information between the above-mentioned IoT components.
Using energy-efficient hardware and software;	
Efficiently managing hardware and software resources and task schedules;	
Implementing power saving methods for virtual machine management.	

As can be seen from the previous tables, there is a wide range of hardware and software solutions for minimizing the negative effects on the environment of using IoT components. These include low energy consumption, limiting non-renewable or polluting resources in building and infrastructure and optimizing production processes across diverse fields. Considering the exponential increase in the number of connected objects expected over the next few years, the effects of these objects on the environment over their life cycle are very important. But the results of studies in this field are positive. A report done by Ericsson (2015) claims that the IoT, through smart transport (1%), smart buildings (1%), smart travel (2%), smart work (2%), smart agriculture and land use (3%), smart services/smart industry (3%) and smart grids, including smart homes (4%), could help to cut up to 63.5 Gt of GHG emissions by 2030, or a total of up to 15%.

The Economic Impact of Green IoT

Green IoT has economic effects both in terms of increasing and decreasing costs and revenues. Some changes can be intuited, while others will emerge in the future. According to data from Cisco Systems, IoT is poised to generate $19 trillion in economic value for businesses and society, as well as cost savings, improved citizen services and increased revenues for governments and other public-sector organizations. (Chambers, 2014) Green IoT creates new sources of revenue for developers and users and has the potential to transform following sectors of the green economy: agriculture, energy supply/renewable energy, fisheries, buildings, forestry, industry/manufacturing, tourism, transport, waste management and water. Businesses will adopt IoT solutions to improve their bottom line by lowering operating costs, increasing productivity and expanding to new markets or developing new product offerings. (Greenough, 2016) But, the IoT is essential for the smart environment. According to Carrino et al. (2016), these technologies allow reliable access to heterogeneous and distributed data and may represent a good solution for the smart cities of the future.

Even without addressing environmental issues directly, the IoT can contribute to protecting the environment through the rigorous monitoring of water and energy consumption, waste management and through intensifying efforts to reduce climate change. The IoT's capacity to increase energy efficiency with smart grids, even if less environmentally-friendly sources are used, leads to cost savings and less CO_2 emissions. In the case of water, the information it provides can help users and different objects to better plan their usage and overall water conservation. In the case of waste management, the IoT helps to measure waste levels in public bins and compact trash, in order to enhance efficiency by planning collection routes where and when pickup is needed. (Adler, 2015) In agriculture, smart farming solutions help farmers to preserve resources and to minimize costs. The IoT has the potential to prevent natural disasters, to support the rational use of water resources, to control the product quality so as not to endanger the health of consumers, etc. All of these are benefits of the IoT. Green IoT, through the development and use of energy-efficient devices, increases these environmental benefits and revenues while decreasing costs. For example, energy-autonomous devices could harvest energy from natural sources and could become energy suppliers for other devices or sub-systems. They could eliminate energy costs for themselves and for other objects.

Increasing the number of IoT devices leads to an increase in the volume of e-waste and to the growth of the e-waste management market. According to a new report from MarketsandMarkets, this market will reach $5.04 billion by 2020, which represents an increase of 20.6% between 2015 and 2020, from $1.66 million in 2014.

The integration of these objects brings with it many challenges and requires significant investments. The EU is investing €192 million in IoT research and innovation from 2014 to 2017. (European Commission, 2016) According to IDC (2017), global

IoT spending will have a compound annual growth rate of 15.6% over the 2015-2020 period, reaching $1.29 trillion in 2020. But this is the price for the more than five billion people and 50 billion things connected (Chambers, 2014) and will bring a compound annual growth rate of at least at 20% over the same period. (Columbus, 2017) Implicitly, a significant percentage of these costs and revenues will lead to environmental protection actions being used for designing and developing green IoT hardware and software. Some of the investments will also be used directly for the production of green IoT devices, which will have a positive impact on the environment.

Conclusion

This paper analyses the two faces of green IoT: reducing the negative effects of IoT use in various fields of activity—green by IoT; and minimizing (even eliminating) the negative effects of IoT devices on the environment—green in IoT. We also presented several economic aspects of green IoT. The analysis of those two perspectives showed that the development of green IoT is a natural consequence of IoT evolution. In many cases, as exemplified in this paper, they naturally contribute to enhancing the relationship with the environment through their destinations.

The IoT Means Too Many Servers

John Harris

John Harris is a columnist at the Guardian, *where he writes about politics and popular culture.*

It was just another moment in this long, increasingly strange summer. I was on a train home from Paddington station, and the carriage's air-conditioning was just about fighting off the heat outside. Most people seemed to be staring at their phones—in many cases, they were trying to stream a World Cup match, as the 4G signal came and went, and Great Western Railway's onboard wifi proved to be maddeningly erratic. The trebly chatter of headphone leakage was constant. And thousands of miles and a few time zones away in Loudoun County, Virginia, one of the world's largest concentrations of computing power was playing its part in keeping everything I saw ticking over, as data from around the world passed back and forth from its vast buildings.

Most of us communicate with this small and wealthy corner of the US every day. Thanks to a combination of factors—its proximity to Washington DC, competitive electricity prices, and its low susceptibility to natural disasters—the county is the home of data centres used by about 3,000 tech companies: huge agglomerations of circuitry, cables and cooling systems that sit in corners of the world most of us rarely see, but that are now at the core of how we live. About 70% of the world's online traffic is reckoned to pass through Loudoun County.

But there is a big problem, centred on a power company called Dominion, which supplies the vast majority of Loudoun County's electricity. According to a 2017 Greenpeace report, only 1% of Dominion's total electricity comes from credibly renewable sources: 2% originates in hydroelectric plants, and the rest is split evenly between coal, gas and nuclear power. Dominion is also in the middle of a huge regional controversy about a proposed pipeline that will carry fracked gas to its power plants, which it says is partly driven by data centres' insatiable appetite for electricity. Clearly, then, the video streams, digital photographs and messaging that pour out of all those servers come with a price.

I was reminded of all this by the recently published book *New Dark Age*, by the British writer James Bridle. He cites a study in Japan that suggests that by 2030, the power requirements of digital services will outstrip the nation's entire current generation capacity. He quotes an American report from 2013—ironically enough, commissioned by coal industry lobbyists—that pointed out that using either a tablet or smartphone to wirelessly watch an hour of video a week used roughly the same amount of electricity (largely consumed at the data-centre end of the process) as two new domestic fridges.

If you worry about climate change and a cause celebre such as the expansion of Heathrow airport, it is worth considering that data centres are set to soon have a bigger carbon footprint than the entire aviation industry. Yet as Bridle points out, even that statistic doesn't quite do justice to some huge potential problems. He mentions the vast amounts of electricity consumed by the operations of the online currency Bitcoin—which, at the height of the speculative frenzies earlier this year, was set to produce an annual amount of carbon dioxide equivalent to 1m transatlantic flights. And he's anxious about what will happen next: "In response to vast increases in data storage and computational capacity in the last decade, the amount of energy used by data centres has doubled every four years, and is expected to triple in the next 10 years."

These changes are partly being driven by the so-called internet of things: the increasing array of everyday devices—from TVs, through domestic security devices, to lighting systems, and countless modes of transport—that constantly emit and receive data. If driverless cars ever arrive in our lives, those same flows will increase hugely. At the same time, the accelerating rollout of the internet and its associated technologies in the developing world will add to the load.

About a decade ago, we were being told to fight climate change by switching off our TVs and stereos. If the battle is now even more urgent, how does it fit with a world in which router lights constantly flicker, and all the devices we own will be in constant, energy-intensive communication with distant mega-computers?

But some good news. Whatever its other ethical contortions, Silicon Valley has an environmental conscience. Facebook has pledged to, sooner or later, power its operations using "100% clean and renewable energy." Google says it has already achieved that goal. So does Apple. Yet even if you factor in efficiency improvements, beneath many of these claims lies a reality in which the vast and constant demand for power means such companies inevitably use energy generated by fossil fuels, and then atone for it using the often questionable practice of carbon offsetting.

And among the big tech corporations, there is one big focus of worry: Amazon, whose ever-expanding cloud computing wing, Amazon Web Services, offers "the on-demand delivery of computer power, database storage … and other IT resources" and provides most of the computing power behind Netflix. This sits at the heart of data centres' relentless expansion. Green campaigners bemoan the fact that the details of AWS's electricity consumption and its carbon footprint remain under wraps; on its corporate website, the story of its use of renewable energy suddenly stops in 2016.

Besides, for all their power, even the most enlightened US giants obviously command only part of a global industry. To quote from that Greenpeace report: "Among emerging Chinese internet giants such as Baidu, Tencent and Alibaba, the silence on energy performance still remains. Neither the public nor customers are able to obtain any information about their electricity use and CO_2 target." Irrespective of the good work carried out by some tech giants, and whether or not you take seriously projections that the entire communication technology industry could account for up to 14% of carbon emissions by 2040, one stark fact remains:

the vast majority of electricity used in the world's data centres comes from non-renewable sources, and as their numbers rapidly increase, there are no guarantees that this will change.

On the fringes of the industry, a few voices have been heard describing the kind of future at which most of us—expecting everything streamed as a right—would balk. They talk about eventually rationing internet use, insisting that people send black and white images, or forcibly pushing them away from binge-streaming videos. Their basic point, it seems, chimes with those occasions when the smartphone in your pocket starts to suddenly heat up: a metaphor for our warming planet, and the fact that even the most well-intentioned corporations may yet find that their supposedly unlimited digital delights are, in the dictionary definition of the term, unsustainable.

CHAPTER 4

Is Data Safe Inside the Internet of Things?

Overview: The Value of Data in the IoT

Patrick McFadin

Patrick McFadin is a spokesman for Apache Cassandra, an open-source platform designed to handle large amounts of data.

The Internet of Things means different things to different people. To vendors, it's the latest in a slew of large-scale trends to affect their enterprise customers, and the latest marketing bandwagon they have to consider. To enterprise organizations, it's still a jumble of technical standards, conflicting opinions and big potential. For developers, it's a big opportunity to put together the right mix of tools and technologies, and probably something they are already doing under another name. Understanding how these technologies work together on a technical level is becoming important, and will provide more opportunities to use software design as part of the overall business.

As Internet of Things projects go from concepts to reality, one of the biggest challenges is how the data created by devices will flow through the system. How many devices will be creating information? How will they send that information back? Will you be capturing that data in real time, or in batches? What role will analytics play in the future?

These questions have to be asked in the design phase. From the organizations that I have spoken to, this preparation phase is essential to make sure you use the right tools from the start.

Sending the Data

It is helpful to think about the data created by a device in three stages. Stage one is the initial creation, which takes place on the device, and then sent over the Internet. Stage two is how the central

"Internet of Things: Where Does the Data Go?" by Patrick McFadin, Apache Cassandra, Condé Nast. Reprinted by permission.

system collects and organizes that data. Stage three is the ongoing use of that data for the future.

For smart devices and sensors, each event can and will create data. This information can then be sent over the network back to the central application. At this point, one must decide which standard the data will be created in and how it will be sent over the network. For delivering this data back, MQTT, HTTP and CoAP are the most common standard protocols used. Each of these has its benefits and use cases.

HTTP provides a suitable method for providing data back and forth between devices and central systems. Originally developed for the client-server computing model, today it supports everyday web browsing through to more specialist services around Internet of Things devices too. While it meets the functionality requirements for sending data, HTTP includes a lot more data around the message in its headers. When you are working in low bandwidth conditions, this can make HTTP less suitable.

MQTT was developed as a protocol for machine-to-machine and Internet of Things deployments. It is based on a publish/subscribe model for delivering messages out from the device back to a central system that acts as a broker, where they can then be delivered back out to all of the other systems that will consume them. New devices or services can simply connect to the broker as they need messages. MQTT is lighter than HTTP in terms of message size, so it is more useful for implementations where bandwidth is a potential issue. However, it does not include encryption as standard so this has to be considered separately.

CoAP is another standard developed for low-power, low-bandwidth environments. Rather than being designed for a broker system like MQTT, CoAP is more aimed at one-to-one connections. It is designed to meet the requirements of REST design by providing a way to interface with HTTP, but still meet the demands of low-power devices and environments.

Each of these protocols support taking information or updates from the individual device and sending it over to a central location.

However, where there is a greater opportunity is how that data is then stored and used in the future. There are two main concerns here: how the data is acted upon as it comes into the application, and how it is stored for future use.

Storing the Data

Across the Internet of Things, devices create data that is sent to the main application to be sent on, consumed and used. Depending on the device, the network and power consumption restraints, data can be sent in real time, or in batches at any time. However, the real value is derived from the order in which data points are created.

This time-series data has to be accurate for Internet of Things applications. If not, then it compromises the very aims of the applications themselves. Take telemetry data from vehicles. If the order of data is not completely aligned and accurate, then it points to potentially different results when analyzed. If a certain part starts to fail in particular conditions—for example, a temperature drop at the same time as a specific level of wear—then these conditions have to be accurately reflected in the data that is coming through, or it will lead to false results.

Time-series data can be created as events take place around the device and then sent. This use of real-time information provides a complete record for each device, as it happens. Alternatively, it can be collated as data is sent across in batches—the historical record of data will be there, it just isn't available in real time. This is common with devices where battery life is a key requirement over the need for data to be delivered in real time. Either way, the fundamental requirement is that each transaction on each device is put in at the right time-stamp for sorting and alignment. If you are looking at doing this in real time with hundreds of thousands or potentially millions of devices, then write-speed at the database level is an essential consideration.

Each write has to be taken as it is received from the device itself and put into the database. For more traditional relational database technologies, this can be a limiting factor, as it is possible for write-requests to go beyond what the database was built for. When you have to have all the data from devices in order to create accurate and useful information, this potential loss can have a big impact. For the organizations that I have spoken to around Internet of Things projects, NoSQL platforms like Cassandra provide a better fit for their requirements.

Part of this is due to the sheer volume of writes that something like Cassandra is capable of; even with millions of devices that creating data all the time, the database is designed to ingest that much data as it is created. However, it is also due to how databases themselves are designed. Traditional databases have a primary-replica arrangement, where the lead database server will handle all the transactions and synchronously pass them along to other servers if required. This leads to problems in the event of an outage or server failure, as a new primary has to be put into place leading to a potential data loss.

For properly configured distributed database systems like Cassandra, there is no "primary" server that is in charge; each node within a cluster can handle transactions as they come in, and the full record is maintained over time. Even if a server fails, or a node is removed due to loss of network connectivity, the rest of the cluster can continue to process data as it comes in. For time-series data, this is especially valuable as it means that there should be no loss of data in the list of transactions over time.

Analyzing the Data

Once you have this store of time-series data, the next opportunity is to look for trends over time. Analyzing time-series data provides the opportunity to create more value for the owners of the devices involved, or carry out automated tasks based on a certain set of conditions being met. The typical example is the Internet-connected fridge that realizes it is out of milk; however, Internet of Things data is more valuable when linked to larger private or public benefits, and with more complex condition sets that have to be met. Traffic analysis, utility networks and use of power across real estate locations are all concerned with consuming data from multiple devices in order to spot trends and save money or time.

In this environment, it's helpful to think about when the results of the analytics will be required: is there an immediate, near real-time need for analysis, or is this a historic requirement? The popularity of Apache Spark for analysis of big data and Spark streaming in near real time has continued to grow, and when combined with the likes of Cassandra it can provide developers with the ability to process and analyze large, fast-moving data sets alongside each other.

However, this is not just about what is taking place right now. The value from time-series data can come over time just as well. As an example, i2O Water in the UK looks at information around water pressure, taken from devices that are embedded in water distribution networks around the world. This data has been gathered over two years and is stored in a Cassandra cluster. The company uses this information for its analytics and to alert customers around where maintenance might be needed.

This data has its own value for the company. It has a ready-made source of modeling and analytics information for customers that can be used around new products too. This is down to the interesting way that the company has architected its applications in a modular fashion; when a new module or service is added, the time-series data can be "played" into the system as if the data was being created. This can then be used for analytics and to show how the devices on the water network would have reacted to the variations in pressure or other sensor data during that time.

For i2O Water, the opportunity here is to add services that demonstrate more value back to the utility companies that are customers. The value of water will only increase as more people need access, which in turn makes accurate and timely data more valuable. This is a good example of how connecting devices and data can improve lives as well as create new opportunities for the companies involved.

The ability to look back at time-series data has the most far-reaching consequences for the Internet of Things as a whole. Whether it's for private sector gain or public sector good, the design of the application and how that data is stored over time is essential to understand. When designing for the Internet of Things, the role of distributed systems that can keep up with the sheer amount of data being created is also important.

Blockchain Will Make the IoT Secure

Nir Kshetri

Nir Kshetri teaches at the University of North Carolina–Greensboro's Department of Management.

The world is full of connected devices—and more are coming. In 2017, there were an estimated 8.4 billion internet-enabled thermostats, cameras, streetlights and other electronics. By 2020 that number could exceed 20 billion, and by 2030 there could be 500 billion or more. Because they'll all be online all the time, each of those devices—whether a voice-recognition personal assistant or a pay-by-phone parking meter or a temperature sensor deep in an industrial robot—will be vulnerable to a cyberattack and could even be part of one.

Today, many "smart" internet-connected devices are made by large companies with well-known brand names, like Google, Apple, Microsoft and Samsung, which have both the technological systems and the marketing incentive to fix any security problems quickly. But that's not the case in the increasingly crowded world of smaller internet-enabled devices, like light bulbs, doorbells and even packages shipped by UPS. Those devices—and their digital "brains"—are typically made by unknown companies, many in developing countries, without the funds or ability—or the brand-recognition need—to incorporate strong security features.

Insecure "internet of things" devices have already contributed to major cyber-disasters, such as the October 2016 cyberattack on internet routing company Dyn that took down more than 80 popular websites and stalled internet traffic across the US. The solution to this problem, in my view as a scholar of "internet of things" technology, blockchain systems and cybersecurity, could be

"Using Blockchain to Secure the 'Internet of Things,'" by Nir Kshetri, The Conversation Media Group Ltd, March 7, 2018. https://theconversation.com/using-blockchain-to -secure-the-internet-of-things-90002. Licensed under CC BY-ND 4.0.

a new way of tracking and distributing security software updates using blockchains.

Making Security a Priority

Today's big technology companies work hard to keep users safe, but they have set themselves a daunting task: Thousands of complex software packages running on systems all over the world will invariably have errors that make them vulnerable to hackers. They also have teams of researchers and security analysts who try to identify and fix flaws before they cause problems.

When those teams find out about vulnerabilities (whether from their own or others' work, or from users' reports of malicious activity), they are well positioned to program updates, and to send them out to users. These companies' computers, phones and even many software programs connect periodically to their manufacturers' sites to check for updates, and can download and even install them automatically.

Beyond the staffing needed to track problems and create fixes, that effort requires enormous investment. It requires software to respond to the automated inquiries, storage space for new versions of software, and network bandwidth to send it all out to millions of users quickly. That's how people's iPhones, PlayStations and copies of Microsoft Word all stay fairly seamlessly up to date with security fixes.

None of that is happening with the manufacturers of the next generation of internet devices. Take, for example, Hangzhou Xiongmai Technology, based near Shanghai, China. Xiongmai makes internet-connected cameras and accessories under its brand and sells parts to other vendors.

Many of its products—and those of many other similar companies—contained administrative passwords that were set in the factory and were difficult or impossible to change. That left the door open for hackers to connect to Xiongmai-made devices, enter the preset password, take control of webcams or other devices, and generate enormous amounts of malicious internet traffic.

When the problem—and its global scope—became clear, there was little Xiongmai and other manufacturers could do to update their devices. The ability to prevent future cyberattacks like that depends on creating a way these companies can quickly, easily and cheaply issue software updates to customers when flaws are discovered.

A Potential Answer

Put simply, a blockchain is a transaction-recording computer database that's stored in many different places at once. In a sense, it's like a public bulletin board where people can post notices of transactions. Each post must be accompanied by a digital signature, and can never be changed or deleted.

I'm not the only person suggesting using blockchain systems to improve internet-connected devices' security. In January 2017, a group including US networking giant Cisco, German engineering firm Bosch, Bank of New York Mellon, Chinese electronics maker Foxconn, Dutch cybersecurity company Gemalto and a number of blockchain startup companies formed to develop just such a system.

It would be available for device makers to use in place of creating their own software update infrastructure the way the tech giants have. These smaller companies would have to program their products to check in with a blockchain system periodically to see if there was new software. Then they would securely upload their updates as they developed them. Each device would have a strong cryptographic identity, to ensure the manufacturer is communicating with the right device. As a result, device makers and their customers would know the equipment would efficiently keep its security up to date.

These sorts of systems would have to be easy to program into small devices with limited memory space and processing power. They would need standard ways to communicate and authenticate updates, to tell official messages from hackers' efforts. Existing blockchains, including Bitcoin SPV and Ethereum Light Client Protocol, look promising. And blockchain innovators will continue to find better ways, making it even easier for billions of "internet of things" devices to check in and update their security automatically.

The Importance of External Pressure

It will not be enough to develop blockchain-based systems that are capable of protecting "internet of things" devices. If the devices' manufacturers don't actually use those systems, everyone's cybersecurity will still be at risk. Companies that make cheap devices with small profit margins, so they won't add these layers of protection without help and support from the outside. They'll need technological assistance and pressure from government regulations and consumer expectations to make the shift from their current practices.

If it's clear their products won't sell unless they're more secure, the unknown "internet of things" manufacturers will step up and make users and the internet as a whole safer.

If Challenges Are Addressed, the IoT Can Reach Its Full Potential

Sachin Kumar, Prayag Tiwari, and Mikhail Zymbler

Sachin Kumar is affiliated with the Department of Computer Science at South Ural State University. Prayag Tiwari is affiliated with the Department of Information Engineering at the University of Padova. Mikhail Zymbler is affiliated with the Department of Computer Science at South Ural State University.

The Internet of Things (IoT) is an emerging paradigm that enables the communication between electronic devices and sensors through the internet in order to facilitate our lives. IoT uses smart devices and the internet to provide innovative solutions to various challenges and issues related to various business, governmental and public/private industries across the world. IoT is progressively becoming an important aspect of our life that can be sensed everywhere around us. In whole, IoT is an innovation that puts together an extensive variety of smart systems, frameworks and intelligent devices and sensors. Moreover, it takes advantage of quantum and nanotechnology in terms of storage, sensing and processing speed, which were not conceivable beforehand. Extensive research studies have been done and are available in terms of scientific articles, press reports both on the internet and in the form of printed materials to illustrate the potential effectiveness and applicability of IoT transformations. It could be utilized as a preparatory work before making novel innovative business plans while considering security, assurance and interoperability.

A great transformation can be observed in our daily routine life along with the increasing involvement of IoT devices and technology. One such development of IoT is the concept of Smart

"Internet of Things Is a Revolutionary Approach for Future Technology Enhancement: A Review," by Sachin Kumar, Prayag Tiwari, and Mikhail Zymbler, *Journal of Big Data*, December 9, 2019. https://journalofbigdata.springeropen.com/articles/10.1186/s40537 -019-0268-2#rightslink. Licensed under CC BY 4.0 International.

Home Systems (SHS) and appliances that consist of internet based devices, automation systems for homes and reliable energy management systems. Besides, another important achievement of IoT is Smart Health Sensing System (SHSS). SHSS incorporates small intelligent equipment and devices to support the health of the human being. These devices can be used both indoors and outdoors to check and monitor the different health issues and fitness level or the amount of calories burned in the fitness center etc. Also, it is being used to monitor critical health conditions in hospitals and trauma centers as well. Hence, it has changed the entire scenario of the medical domain by facilitating it with high technology and smart devices. Moreover, IoT developers and researchers are actively involved to uplift the lifestyle of the disabled and senior age group people. IoT has shown a drastic performance in this area and has provided a new direction for the normal life of such people. As these devices and equipment are very cost effective in terms of development cost and easily available within a normal price range, most of the people are availing them. Thanks to IoT, they can live a normal life. Another important aspect of our life is transportation. IoT has brought up some new advancements to make it more efficient, comfortable and reliable. Intelligent sensors and drone devices are now controlling the traffic at different signalized intersections across major cities. In addition, vehicles are being launched in markets with pre-installed sensing devices that are able to sense the upcoming heavy traffic congestions on the map and may suggest to you another route with low traffic congestion. Therefore IoT has a lot to serve in various aspects of life and technology. We may conclude that IoT has a lot of scope both in terms of technology enhancement and facilitating humankind.

IoT has also shown its importance and potential in the economic and industrial growth of a developing region. Also, in trade and stock exchange markets, it is being considered as a revolutionary step. However, security of data and information is an important concern and highly desirable, which is a major challenging issue to deal with. The internet being a large source of security threats and cyber-attacks has opened the various doors for hackers and thus made the data and information insecure. However, IoT is committed to provide the best possible solutions to deal with security issues of data and information. Hence, the most important concern of IoT in trade and economy is security. Therefore, the development of a secure path for collaboration between social networks and privacy concerns is a hot topic in IoT, and IoT developers are working hard on this.

[...]

IoT Architecture and Technologies

The IoT architecture consists of five important layers that define all the functionalities of IoT systems. These layers are the perception layer, network layer, middleware layer, application layer, and business layer. At the bottom of IoT architecture, the perception layer exists that consists of physical devices, i.e. sensors, RFID chips, barcodes, etc., and other physical objects connected in IoT networks. These devices collect information in order to deliver it to the network layer. The network layer works as a transmission medium to deliver the information from perception layer to the information processing system. This transmission of information may use any wired/wireless medium along with 3G/4G, Wi-Fi, Bluetooth, etc. The next layer is known as the middleware layer. The main task of this layer is to process the information received from the network layer and make decisions based on the results achieved from ubiquitous computing. Next, this processed information is used by the application layer for global device management. On the top of the architecture, there is a business layer which controls the overall IoT system, its applications and services. The business layer visualizes the information and statistics received from the application layer and further uses this knowledge to plan future targets and strategies. Furthermore, the IoT architectures can be modified according to the needs and application domain. Besides layered framework, IoT systems consist of several functional blocks that support various IoT activities, such as sensing mechanism, authentication and identification, control and management.

There are several important functional blocks responsible for I/O operations, connectivity issues, processing, audio/video monitoring and storage management. All these functional blocks together incorporate an efficient IoT system and are important for optimum performance. Although, there are several reference architectures proposed with the technical specifications, but these are still far from the standard architecture that is suitable for global IoT. Therefore, a suitable architecture still needs to be designed that could satisfy the global IoT needs. IoT gateways have an important role in IoT communication as they allow connectivity between IoT servers and IoT devices related to several applications.

Scalability, modularity, interoperability and openness are the key design issues for an efficient IoT architecture in a heterogeneous environment. The IoT architecture must be designed with an objective to fulfil the requirements of cross domain interactions, multi-system integration with the potential of simple and scalable management functionalities, big data analytics and storage, and user friendly applications. Also, the architecture should be able to scale-up the functionality and add some intelligence and automation among the IoT devices in the system.

Moreover, the increasing amount of massive data being generated through the communication between IoT sensors and devices is a new challenge. Therefore, an efficient architecture is required to deal with the massive amount of streaming data in IoT systems. Two popular IoT system architectures are cloud and fog/edge computing that support the handling, monitoring and analysis of huge amounts of data in IoT systems. Therefore, a modern IoT architecture can be defined as a 4 stage architecture.

In stage 1 of the architecture, sensors and actuators play an important role. The real world is comprised of environment, humans, animals, electronic gadgets, smart vehicles, and buildings, etc. Sensors detect the signals and data flow from these real world entities and transform them into data that can further be used for analysis. Moreover, actuators are able to intervene the reality, i.e., to control the temperature of the room, to slow down the vehicle speed, to turn off the music and light, etc. Therefore, stage 1 assists in collecting data from the real world that could be useful for further analysis. Stage 2 is responsible for collaborating with sensors and actuators along with gateways and data acquisition systems. In this stage, the massive amount of data generated in stage 1 is aggregated and optimized in a structured way suitable for processing. Once the massive amount of data is aggregated and structured, then it is ready to be passed to stage 3, which is edge computing. Edge computing can be defined as an open architecture in distributed fashion that allows use of IoT technologies and massive computing power from different locations worldwide. It is a very powerful approach for streaming data processing and thus suitable for IoT systems. In stage 3, edge computing technologies deal with massive amounts of data and provide various functionalities such as visualization, integration of data from other sources, analysis using machine learning methods, etc. The last stage comprises several important activities such as in-depth processing and analysis, sending feedback to improve the precision and accuracy of the entire system. Everything at this stage will be performed on a cloud server or data centre. Big data frameworks such as Hadoop and Spark may be utilized to handle this large streaming data and machine learning approaches can be used to develop better prediction models which could help in a more accurate and reliable IoT system to meet the demand of present time.

Major Key Issues and Challenges of IoT

The involvement of IoT-based systems in all aspects of human lives and various technologies involved in data transfer between embedded devices made it complex and gave rise to several issues and challenges. These issues are also a challenge for the IoT developers in the advanced smart tech society. As technology is growing, challenges and need for advanced IoT systems are also growing. Therefore, IoT developers need to think of new issues arising and should provide solutions for them.

Security and Privacy Issues

One of the most important and challenging issues in the IoT is security and privacy due to several threats, cyber attacks, risks and vulnerabilities. The issues that give rise to device level privacy are insufficient authorization and authentication, insecure software, firmware, web interface and poor transport layer encryption. Security and privacy issues are very important parameters to develop confidence in IoT systems with respect to various aspects. Security mechanisms must be embedded at every layer of IoT architecture to prevent security threats and attacks. Several protocols are developed and efficiently deployed on every layer of communication channel to ensure the security and privacy in IoT-based systems. Secure Socket Layer (SSL) and Datagram Transport Layer Security (DTLS) are two of the cryptographic protocols that are implemented between transport and application layer to provide security solutions in various IoT systems. However, some IoT applications require different methods to ensure the security in communication between IoT devices. Besides this, if communication takes place using wireless technologies within the IoT system, it becomes more vulnerable to security risks. Therefore, certain methods should be deployed to detect malicious actions and for self healing or recovery. Privacy on the other hand is another important concern which allows users to feel secure and comfortable while using IoT solutions. Therefore, it is required to maintain the authorization and authentication over a secure network to establish the communication between trusted parties. Another issue is the different privacy policies for different objects communicating within the IoT system. Therefore, each object should be able to verify the privacy policies of other objects in the IoT system before transmitting the data.

Interoperability/Standard Issues

Interoperability is the feasibility to exchange the information among different IoT devices and systems. This exchange of information does not rely on the deployed software and hardware. The interoperability issue arises due to the heterogeneous nature of different technology and solutions used for IoT development. The four interoperability levels are technical, semantic, syntactic and organizational. Various functionalities are being provided by IoT systems to improve the interoperability that ensures communication between different objects in a heterogeneous environment. Additionally, it is possible to merge different IoT platforms based on their functionalities to provide various solutions for IoT users. Considering interoperability an important issue, researchers approved several solutions that are also known as interoperability handling approaches. These solutions could be adapter/gateway based, virtual networks/overlay based, service oriented architecture based, etc. Although interoperability handling approaches ease some pressure on IoT systems, there are still certain challenges that remain with interoperability that could be a scope for future studies.

Ethics, Law and Regulatory Rights

Another issue for IoT developers is ethics, law and regulatory rights. There are certain rules and regulations to maintain the standard, moral values and to prevent people from violating them. Ethics and law are very similar terms with the only difference that ethics are standards that people believe and laws are certain restrictions decided by the government. However, both ethics and laws are designed to maintain the standard, quality and prevent people from illegal use. With the development of IoT, several real life problems are solved but it has also given rise to critical ethical and legal challenges. Data security, privacy protection, trust and safety, data usability are some of those challenges. It has also been observed that the majority of IoT users are supporting government norms and regulations with respect to data protection, privacy and safety due to the lack of trust in IoT devices. Therefore, this issue must be taken into consideration to maintain and improve the trust among people for the use of IoT devices and systems.

Scalability, Availability and Reliability

A system is scalable if it is possible to add new services, equipment and devices without degrading its performance. The main issue with IoT is to support a large number of devices with different memory, processing, storage power and bandwidth. Another important issue that must be taken into consideration is the availability. Scalability and availability both should be deployed together in the layered framework of IoT. A great example of scalability is cloud based IoT systems which provide sufficient support to scale the IoT network by adding up new devices, storage and processing power as required.

However, this global distributed IoT network gives rise to a new research paradigm to develop a smooth IoT framework that satisfies global needs. Another key challenge is the availability of resources to the authentic objects regardless of their location and time of the requirement. In a distributed fashion, several small IoT networks are timely attached to the global IoT platforms to utilize their resources and services. Therefore, availability is an important concern. Due to the use of different data transmission channels, i.e. satellite communication, some services and availability of resources may be interrupted. Therefore, an independent and reliable data transmission channel is required for uninterrupted availability of resources and services.

Quality of Service (QoS)

Quality of Service (QoS) is another important factor for IoT. QoS can be defined as a measure to evaluate the quality, efficiency and performance of IoT devices, systems and architecture. The important and required QoS metrics for IoT applications are reliability, cost, energy consumption, security, availability and service time. A smarter IoT ecosystem must fulfill the requirements of QoS standards. Also, to ensure the reliability of any IoT service and device, its QoS metrics must be defined first. Further, users may also be able to specify their needs and requirements accordingly. Several approaches can be deployed for QoS assessment, however as mentioned by White et al. there is a trade-off between quality factors and approaches. Therefore, good quality models must be deployed to overcome this trade-off. There are certain good quality models available in literature such as ISO/IEC25010 and OASIS-WSQM which can be used to evaluate the approaches used for QoS assessment. These models provide a wide range of quality factors that is quite sufficient for QoS assessment for IoT services.

Major IoT Applications

Emerging Economy, Environmental and Health Care

IoT is completely devoted to providing emerging public and financial benefits and development to society and people. This includes a wide range of public facilities, i.e. economic development, water quality maintenance, well-being, industrialization, etc. Overall, IoT is working hard to accomplish the social, health and economic goals of the United Nations. Environmental sustainability is another important concern. IoT developers must be concerned about environmental impact of the IoT systems and devices to overcome the negative impact. Energy consumption by IoT devices is one of the challenges related to environmental impact. Energy consumption is increasing at a high rate due to internet enabled services and cutting-edge devices. This area needs research for the development of high quality materials in order to create new IoT devices with lower energy consumption rates. Also, green technologies can be adopted to create energy efficient devices for future use. It is not only environmental friendly but also advantageous for human health. Researchers and engineers are engaged in developing highly efficient IoT devices to monitor several health issues, such as diabetes, obesity or depression. Several issues related to the environment, energy and health care are considered by several studies.

Smart City, Transport and Vehicles

IoT is transforming the traditional civil structure of society into high tech structure with the concept of smart cities, smart homes and smart vehicles and transport. Rapid improvements are being done with the help of supporting technologies such as machine learning, natural language processing to understand the need and use of technology at home. Various technologies such as cloud server technology and wireless sensor networks must be used with IoT servers to provide an efficient smart city. Another important issue to think about is the environmental aspect of smart cities. Therefore, energy efficient technologies and Green technologies should also be considered for the design and planning of smart city infrastructure. Further, smart devices which are being incorporated into newly launched vehicles are able to detect traffic congestion on the road and thus can suggest an optimum alternate route to the driver. This can help to lower the congestion in the city. Furthermore, smart devices with optimum cost should be designed to be incorporated in all range vehicles to monitor the activity of the engine. IoT is also very effective in maintaining the vehicle's health. Self-driving cars have the potential to communicate with other self-driving vehicles by the means of intelligent sensors. This would make the traffic flow smoother than human-driven cars that are used to drive in a stop and go manner. This procedure will take time to be implemented all over the world. Till that time, IoT devices can help by sensing traffic congestion ahead and can take appropriate actions. Therefore, a transport manufacturing company should incorporate IoT devices into their manufactured vehicles to provide its advantage to society.

Agriculture and Industry Automation

The world's growing population is estimated to reach approximately 10 billion by 2050. Agriculture plays an important role in our lives. In order to feed such a massive population, we need to advance the current agriculture approaches. Therefore, there is a need to combine agriculture with technology so that the production can be improved in an efficient way. Greenhouse technology is one of the possible approaches in this direction. It provides a way to control the environmental parameters in order to improve the production. However, manual control of this technology is less effective, needs manual efforts and cost, and results in energy loss and less production. With the advancement of IoT, smart devices and sensors make it easier to control the climate inside the chamber and monitor the process which results in energy saving and improved production. Automation of industries is another advantage of IoT. IoT has been providing game changing solutions for factory digitalization, inventory management, quality control, logistics and supply chain optimization and management.

Importance of Big Data Analytics in IoT

An IoT system comprises a huge number of devices and sensors that communicate with each other. With the extensive growth and expansion of IoT networks, the number of these sensors and devices are increasing rapidly. These devices communicate with each other and transfer a massive amount of data over the internet. This data is very huge and streaming every second and thus qualified to be called big data. Continuous expansion of IoT-based networks gives rise to complex issue such as management and collection of data, storage and processing and analytics. IoT big data framework for smart buildings is very useful to deal with several issues of smart buildings such as managing oxygen level, to measure the smoke/ hazardous gases and luminosity. Such framework is capable to collect the data from the sensors installed in the buildings and perform data analytics for decision making. Moreover, industrial production can be improved using an IoT-based cyber physical system that is equipped with information analysis and knowledge acquisition techniques. Traffic congestion is an important issue with smart cities. The real time traffic information can be collected through IoT devices and sensors installed in traffic signals and this information can be analyzed in an IoT-based traffic management system. In health care analysis, the IoT sensors used with patients generate a lot of information about the health condition of patients every second. This large amount of information needs to be integrated at one database and must be processed in real time to make quick decision with high accuracy, and big data technology is the best solution for this job. IoT along with big data analytics can also help to transform the traditional approaches used in manufacturing industries into modern ones. The sensing devices generate information which can be analyzed using big data approaches and may help in various decision making tasks. Furthermore, use of cloud computing and analytics can benefit energy development and conservation with reduced cost and customer satisfaction. IoT devices generate a huge amount of streaming data which needs to be stored effectively and needs further analysis for decision making in real time. Deep learning is very effective to deal with such a large amount information and can provide results with high accuracy. Therefore, IoT, big data analytics and deep learning together are very important to develop a high tech society.

Conclusions

Recent advancements in IoT have drawn the attention of researchers and developers worldwide. IoT developers and researchers are working together to extend the technology on a large scale and to benefit society to the highest possible level. However, improvements are possible only if we consider the various issues and shortcomings in the present technical approaches. In this survey article, we presented several issues and challenges that IoT developers must take into account to develop an improved model. Also, important application areas of IoT are also discussed where IoT developers and researchers are engaged. IoT not only provides services but also generates a huge amount of data. Hence, the importance of big data analytics is also discussed which can provide accurate decisions that could be utilized to develop an improved IoT system.

Blockchain Technology Requires Permissionless Innovation to Flourish

Nur Baysal

Nur Baysal is a research associate at the Competitive Enterprise Institute and Technology and Disruption Fellow at the Consumer Choice Center.

Blockchain has been hitting the headlines recently. Once regarded as a niche interest for technologically experienced libertarians and other computer nerds, cryptocurrencies like Bitcoin are something that most people have probably heard of by now.

Not all of the news has been positive—headlines about things such as market manipulation, ICO frauds, and bans of crypto exchanges in countries like China have generated some substantive wariness. With such a plethora of negative stories around, some might be outright dismissive of the whole technology.

They shouldn't be.

Dismissing a technology that is still in its infancy because of either price volatility or individual acts of fraud is not just closed-minded. It fosters an attitude that thwarts us from learning more about the myriad use cases of the blockchain. Most importantly, a default attitude of skepticism might hinder transformative advancements of blockchain technology in the future, many of which we currently cannot know.

Blockchain Technology Is Gaining Traction

Blockchain innovation is not just limited to cryptocurrencies. Instead, the technology seeks to disrupt a wide span of industries. The use cases of distributed ledger technology span from delivering aid efficiently to refugees, using blockchain to build a digital identity, enabling scientists to use your safely stored genomic data, and a multitude of other fields of application.

These use cases have already started to get noticed by some of the most influential corporations of our time. The Enterprise Ethereum Alliance (EEA), an association of leading Fortune 500 enterprises, startups, and academics, has been created to provide industry leaders with knowledge on how to harness the benefits of Ethereum's smart contract technology for their businesses. EEA members include Intel, Microsoft, J.P. Morgan, Chase, and Cisco Systems.

Another cryptocurrency, Stellar Lumens (XLM/STR), secured a prominent partnership with technology giant IBM in October. XLM is an open-source protocol for exchanging money that aims to increase the speed of payments. According to Michael Dowling, Chief Architect for Blockchain Financial Services at IBM, Stellar Lumens is already directly or indirectly deployed by over 14 institutions.

Permissionless Innovation vs. the Precautionary Principle

None of these use cases were obvious or planned when the pseudonymous author(s) of the Bitcoin white paper introduced the first application of blockchain technology in 2008. Had blockchain been stifled with a "permissioned," top-down regulatory approach, there would have been no room left for innovative exploration. Consequently, many of these revolutionary ideas would never have emerged.

If we want blockchain technology to continue producing disruptive ideas in the future, we need to change our default attitude of skepticism to that of a strong support for technological change. This goes beyond adopting a regulatory framework that is friendly toward technological change. Beyond specific policy proposals, we need to embrace a vision that cultivates a strong support of technological disruption.

In other words, we should give up the precautionary principle and, instead, adopt a culture of permissionless innovation for technological change. In its essence, the precautionary principle proclaims that the introduction of a technology whose ultimate effects are unknown should be resisted. To illustrate this with a recent development, gene-editing techniques such as CRISPR/Cas9 are currently facing calls for regulations due to ethical concerns.

While the precautionary principle fosters a cautious and conservative relationship towards technological disruption, a mindset of permissionless innovation makes us open-minded toward any such change *by default*, with possible criticism and calls for regulations coming later.

The *default setting* of our mind is what's crucial here. Permissionless innovation is not about letting any destructive technology have its way without any regulations. Most technologies have the potential to cause harm. We should carefully listen to Nick Bostrom and others when it comes to possible dangers by AI, for instance.

Rather, the core principle of permissionless innovation is the idea that technological change is generally beneficial towards humanity. When in doubt, we should thus provide entrepreneurs enough room for creative exploration. Enforcing restrictive regulatory barriers is especially bad for new technologies since it hinders the development of ideas that were unforeseen when the technology was just established. As Adam Thierer notes in an essay on his book *Permissionless Innovation: The Continuing Case for Comprehensive Technological Freedom:*

> Permissionless innovation is about the creativity of the human mind to run wild in its inherent curiosity and inventiveness, even when it disrupts certain cultural norms or economic business models. It is that unhindered freedom to experiment that ushered in many of the remarkable technological advances of modern times. In particular, all the digital devices, systems and networks that we now take for granted came about because innovators were at liberty to let their minds run wild.

A recent example of the benefits that permissionless innovation can bring about is the Internet of Things (IoT). Put simply, IoT aims to create a multi-layered network that connects vehicles, home appliances, and almost any physical device to the internet. It consequently enables physical objects to be remotely controlled through existing networks. As a result, the integration of physical and computer-based systems is improved and runs more efficiently. Through this, barriers such as physical distance and direct human intervention are overcome.

The sheer diversity of different products that can take advantage of IoT technology could hardly have been planned in a "permissioned," restricted regulatory framework. Similar to blockchain, the Internet of Things offers exciting future use cases that we cannot predict; some of the most recent developments connect the advantages of IoT to blockchain-like tangle technologies like IOTA's Tangle.

Creating a Culture of Permissionless Innovation— It's About More Than Just Politics

According to Thierer, our public policy vision is currently deeply infused with the precautionary principle. As such, the initial answers to disruptive technologies are regulations that presuppose hypothetical worst-case scenarios. But an attitude in favor of putting brakes on new technologies *by default* is likely to restrict its explorative room for continual improvement. In other words, if you keep expecting worst-case scenarios, you are likely to enforce rules that hinder the development of best-case scenarios. We are more likely to give new technologies enough room for constructive growth if we think they can benefit us in the long-run.

As long as it is solely confined to the realm of public policy, the concept of permissionless innovation will not establish itself as part of our society's framework. More than being chained to the fluctuating game of politics, Adam Thierer notes that permissionless innovation ought to be an "aspirational goal" for the vision of a society. To establish this, society's outlook on technological advancements has to be unapologetically optimistic.

Having firm cultural attitudes and social norms that strengthen this position is of utmost importance. Once we foster what Deirdre McCloskey refers to as "bourgeois virtues"—a positive outlook on innovation through entrepreneurial activity in the market— we can propel further disruptions through new technologies like blockchain, while reaping its continual and transformative benefits in our lives.

The Internet of Things Is Only as Secure as the Internet Is

Temitope Oluwafemi

Temitope Oluwafemi is a solutions architect in the Strategy and Capture Office at Intel Federal LLC.

An ever-increasing number of our consumer electronics is internet-connected. We're living at the dawn of the age of the Internet of Things. Appliances ranging from light switches and door locks, to cars and medical devices boast connectivity in addition to basic functionality.

The convenience can't be beat. But what are the security and privacy implications? Is a patient implanted with a remotely-controllable pacemaker at risk for security compromise? Vice President Dick Cheney's doctors worried enough about an assassination attempt via implant that they disabled his defibrillator's wireless capability. Should we expect capital crimes via hacked internet-enabled devices? Could hackers mount large-scale terrorist attacks? Our research suggests these scenarios are within reason.

Your Car, Out of Your Control

Modern cars are one of the most connected products consumers interact with today. Many of a vehicle's fundamental building blocks—including the engine and brake control modules—are now electronically controlled. Newer cars also support long-range wireless connections via cellular network and Wi-Fi. But hi-tech definitely doesn't mean highly secure.

Our group of security researchers at the University of Washington was able to remotely compromise and control a highly-computerized vehicle. They invaded the privacy of vehicle

"Can a Hacker Stop Your Car or Your Heart? Security and the Internet of Things," by Temitope Oluwafemi, The Conversation, November 18, 2014. Licensed under CC BY-ND 4.0.

occupants by listening in on their conversations. Even more worrisome, they remotely disabled brake and lighting systems and brought the car to a complete stop on a simulated major highway. By exploiting vulnerabilities in critical modules, including the brake systems and engine control, along with in radio and telematics components, our group completely overrode the driver's control of the vehicle. The safety implications are obvious.

This attack raises important questions about how much manufacturers and consumers are willing to sacrifice security and privacy for increased functionality and convenience. Car companies are starting to take these threats seriously, appointing cybersecurity executives. But for the most part, automakers appear to be playing catch-up, dealing with security as an afterthought of the design process.

Home Insecurity

An increasing number of devices around the home are automated and connected to the internet. Many rely on a proprietary wireless communications protocol called Z-Wave.

Two UK researchers exploited security loopholes in Z-Wave's cryptographic libraries—that's the software toolkit that authenticates any device being connected to the home network, among other functions, while providing communication security over the internet. The researchers were able to compromise home automation controllers and remotely-controlled appliances including door locks and alarm systems. Z-Wave's security relied solely on keeping the algorithm a secret from the public, but the researchers were able to reverse engineer the protocol to find weak spots.

Our group was able to compromise Z-Wave controllers via another vulnerability: their web interfaces. Via the web, we could control all home appliances connected to the Z-Wave controller, showing that a hacker could, for instance, turn off the heat in wintertime or watch inhabitants via webcam feeds. We also demonstrated an inherent danger in connecting compact fluorescent lamps (CFL) to a Z-Wave dimmer. These bulbs were not designed with remote manipulations over the internet in mind. We found an attacker could send unique signals to CFLs that would burn them out, emitting sparks that could potentially result in house fires.

Our group also pondered the possibility of a large-scale terrorist attack. The threat model assumes that home automation becomes so ubiquitous that it's a standard feature installed in homes by developers. An attacker could exploit a vulnerability in the automation controllers to turn on power-hungry devices—like HVAC systems—in an entire neighborhood at the same time. With the A/C roaring in every single house, shared power transformers would be overloaded and whole neighborhoods could be knocked off the power grid.

Harnessing Hackers' Knowledge

One of the best practices of designing elegant security solutions is to enlist the help of the security community to find and report weak spots otherwise undetected by the manufacturer. If the internal cryptographic libraries these devices use to obfuscate and recover data, amongst other tasks, are open-source, they can be vetted by the security community. Once issues are found, updates can be pushed to resolve them. Crypto libraries implemented from scratch may be riddled with bugs that the security community would likely find and fix—hopefully before the bad guys find and exploit. Unfortunately, this sound principle has not been strictly adhered to in the world of the Internet of Things.

Third party vendors designed the web interfaces and home appliances with Z-Wave support that our group exploited. We found that, even if a manufacturer has done a very good job and released a secure product, retailers who repackage it with added functionality—like third party software—could introduce vulnerabilities. The end-user can also compromise security by failing to operate the product properly. That's why robust multi-layered security solutions are vital—so a breach can be limited to just a single component, rather than a successful hack into one component compromising the whole system.

Level of Risk

There is one Internet of Things security loophole that law enforcement has taken notice of: thieves' use of scanner boxes that mimic the signals sent out by remote key fobs to break into cars. The other attacks I've described are feasible, but haven't made any headlines yet. Risks today remain low for a variety of reasons. Home automation system attacks at this point appear to be very targeted in nature. Perpetrating them on a neighborhood-wide scale could be a very expensive task for the hacker, thereby decreasing the likelihood of it occurring.

There needs to be a concerted effort to improve security of future devices. Researchers, manufacturers and end users need to be aware that privacy, health and safety can be compromised by increased connectivity. Benefits in convenience must be balanced with security and privacy costs as the Internet of Things continues to infiltrate our personal spaces.

IoT Toys Are Endangering Children

Marie-Helen Maras

Marie-Helen Maras is associate professor in the Department of Security, Fire and Emergency Management at John Jay College of Criminal Justice, City University of New York.

A s Amazon releases an Echo Dot smart-home device aimed at children, it's entering a busy and growing marketplace. More than one-third of US homes with children has at least one "internet of things" connected toy—like a cuddly creature who can listen to and respond to a child's inquiries. Many more of these devices are on the way, around the world and in North America specifically.

These toys wirelessly connect with online databases to recognize voices and images, identifying children's queries, commands and requests and responding to them. They're often billed as improving children's quality of play, providing children with new experiences of collaborative play, and developing children's literacy, numeric and social skills.

Online devices raise privacy concerns for all their users, but children are particularly vulnerable and have special legal protections. Consumer advocates have raised alarms about the toys' insecure wireless internet connections—either directly over Wi-Fi or via Bluetooth to a smartphone or tablet with internet access.

As someone with both academic and practical experience in security, law enforcement and applied technology, I know these fears are not hypothetical. Here are four examples of when internet of things toys put kids' security and privacy at risk.

"4 Ways 'Internet of Things' Toys Endanger Children," by Marie-Helen Maras, The Conversation, May 10, 2018. https://theconversation.com/4-ways-internet-of-things-toys -endanger-children-94092. Licensed under CC BY-ND 4.0.

1. Unsecured Wireless Connections

Some "internet of things" toys can connect to smartphone apps without any form of authentication. So a user can download a free app, find an associated toy nearby, and then communicate directly with the child playing with that toy. In 2015, security researchers discovered that Hello Barbie, an internet-enabled Barbie doll, automatically connected to unsecured Wi-Fi networks that broadcast the network name "Barbie." It would be very simple for an attacker to set up a Wi-Fi network with that name and communicate directly with an unsuspecting child.

The same thing could happen with unsecured Bluetooth connections to the Toy-Fi Teddy, I-Que Intelligent Robot and Furby Connect toys, a British consumer watchdog group revealed in 2017.

The toys' ability to monitor children—even when used as intended and connected to official networks belonging to a toy's manufacturer—violates Germany's anti-surveillance laws. In 2017, German authorities declared the My Friend Cayla doll was an "illegal espionage apparatus," ordering stores to pull it off the shelves and requiring parents to destroy or disable the toys.

Unsecured devices allow attackers to do more than just talk to children: A toy can talk to another internet-connected device, too. In 2017, security researchers hijacked a CloudPets connected stuffed animal and used it to place an order through an Amazon Echo in the same room.

2. Tracking Kids' Movements

Some internet-connected toys have GPS like those in fitness trackers and smartphones, which can also reveal users' locations, even if those users are children. In addition, the Bluetooth communications some toys use can be detected as far away as 30 feet. If someone within that range looks for a Bluetooth device—even if they're only seeking to pair their own headphones with a smartphone—they'll see the toy's name, and know a child is nearby.

For instance, the Consumer Council of Norway found that smartwatches marketed to children were storing and transmitting locations without encryption, allowing strangers to track children's movements. That group issued an alert in its country, but the discovery led authorities in Germany to ban the sale of children's smartwatches.

3. Poor Data Protections

Internet-connected toys have cameras that watch kids and microphones that listen to them, recording what they see and hear. Sometimes they send that information to company servers that analyze the inputs and send back directions on how the toy should respond. But those functions can also be hijacked to listen in on family conversations or take photographs or video of children without the kids or parents ever noticing.

Toy manufacturers don't always ensure the data is stored and transmitted securely, even when laws require it: In 2018, toymaker VTech was fined US$650,000 for failing to fulfill its promises to encrypt private data and for violating US laws protecting children's privacy.

4. Working with Third Parties

Toy companies have also shared the information they collect about kids with other companies—much as Facebook shared its users' data with Cambridge Analytica and other firms.

And they can also surreptitiously share information from third parties with kids. One toy company came under fire, for example, in both Norway and the US for a business relationship with Disney in which the My Friend Cayla doll was programmed to discuss what were described as the doll's favorite Disney movies with kids. Parents weren't told about this arrangement, which critics said amounted to "product placement"-style advertising in a toy.

What Can Parents Do?

In my view, and according to consumer advice from the FBI, parents should carefully research internet-connected toys before buying them, and evaluate their capabilities, functioning, and security and privacy settings before bringing these devices into their homes. Without proper safeguards—by parents, if not toy companies—children are at risk, both individually and through collection of aggregate data about kids' activities.

There Are Interconnected Vulnerabilities of the Internet of Things

UpGuard

UpGuard is a cybersecurity startup that markets security products to companies concerned about outages and breaches.

Cybersecurity compliance standards exist to protect devices, data and people connected to the internet from the myriad threats facing them every day. For example, regulations like the North American Electric Reliability Corporation's (NERC) Critical Infrastructure Protection (CIP) standards ensure businesses operating in the power industry follow certain guidelines with regard to cybersecurity in order to keep the service they provide reliable. Typically, devices that fall within the scope of these regulations include computers, network devices, and other network-connected devices, such as industry-specific tools, card scanners, etc. But what happens when everything is connected to the network?

The basic philosophy behind the Internet of Things (IoT) is that most everything—objects, buildings, vehicles—can and should be connected to the internet. The potential benefits behind doing so are many, but these are just a few:

- Metrics and monitoring. Whether it's your milk getting low, your back door unlocked at night, or the safety of a nuclear reactor, the main idea behind internet-connected devices is to pull data out of the material world and put it into a digital format a human can manipulate to better understand the device in question. In business terms, the applications are nearly endless, as the kind of big data gathered by an IoT system would help increase efficiency, decrease waste and provide objective statistics for use in business decisions.

"Who's Regulating the Internet of Things?" (https://www.upguard.com/articles/security -and-the-internet-of-things), UpGuard, November 20, 2019. Reprinted by permission.

- Remote control. Working with objects in the physical world typically requires the user to share the same physical space as the object. The IoT will make objects (buildings, vehicles…) accessible remotely. The advantages should be obvious here, including freeing people up from physically working in uncomfortable or dangerous environments, management of satellite offices or stations, and most importantly, the possibility to control objects via automation.

- Interconnectivity. If the IoT was just about adding each device to the net as a discrete entity, it wouldn't make much sense. The real power of the IoT comes with interconnecting devices to work together. The IoT is a system, a collection of objects communicating with each other and people. In business terms, this touches everything from manufacturing lines to point of sale devices, to inventory mechanisms. Along with automation, interconnectivity allows the IoT to create a logical network of objects designed around the way people use them.

- Automation. The concept of automation has been at the forefront since the industrial revolution, but automation happens in cycles, just like technology itself. What the IoT ultimately dangles in front of us is an autonomous network of objects, interoperating efficiently without any significant human input. The ramifications of such a system go beyond this survey, but it would be a completely new way of interacting with our environment, like developing a new sense. Initially, of course, the automation will be crude and cumbersome, with interconnectivity limitations determining what can be automated.

- Ease of use. Like smartphones, devices in the IoT will require intuitive, simple interfaces so that non-experts and even non-technologists can take advantage of the benefits. Far from being devices confined to IT shops and enterprise businesses, the IoT depends on popular use, so the innovations that bring it closer to that goal will be defined in large part by their usability.

But the IoT is a double-edged sword, and with these benefits come several drawbacks:

- Surveillance. Metrics and monitoring are great, as long as the data stays in the right hands. Otherwise, that information becomes a vulnerability, allowing third parties to know the intimate details of your environment. Whether hackers, state sponsored agents, or competition, someone could be after that information, because it has value, both to its owner and others.

- Hacking. Again, remote control functionality sounds great, as long as the person doing the remote controlling is an authorized user. Connecting a device to the internet means subjecting that device to the possibility of being taken over and damaged, defaced and/or compromised. This will be as true for IoT devices as it is for laptops and smartphones, so at the scale some IoT evangelists imagine, that's a lot of potential exploitable inroads.

- Cascading failures and vulnerabilities. While interconnectivity increases functionality by linking a series of devices, it also handles failures and vulnerabilities in much the same manner. Discrete objects require more overhead to manage, but are isolated to themselves and their failure only impairs their own functionality. An interconnected system, on the other hand, is a series of dependencies. When one piece goes down, it interrupts a complex chain and renders other, working, parts useless. An old school example of this is exactly why the NERC standards were created in the first place. Likewise, a vulnerability in one piece of an interconnected system can render the entire system vulnerable. It seems a bit silly to imagine someone hacking a wifi light bulb and taking over a house, but that's legitimately within the range of possibilities in the future.

- Faster errors. Every advance in automation is met with an increase in danger when something goes wrong. Much like a cascading failure, when something goes wrong in an automated environment, it interrupts the entire system, often moving the flaw from one stage of automation to the next, compounding the error each time. Furthermore, all of this happens so quickly that it's very difficult for a human operator to make adjustments in time to prevent damage.
- Outsourcing difficulty. Although IoT devices will have slick interfaces, the difficulties they translate still exist, they're just being handled by developers and other technologists at private companies. This means that as people become dependent on easy to use IoT devices, they also become dependent on the companies producing them, on the people working for those companies, on the technical knowledge they possess. This could have serious ramifications in the future, especially imagining an Internet of Living Things, where a conflict of interest could arise between a business' goal and its users' needs.

Given the risks that accompany the IoT, it makes sense that businesses required to follow compliance standards prepare themselves for what's on the horizon. There's time yet to prepare, as the rollout of the IoT will be extremely gradual, coming in stages, waves, with multiple generations of technology co-existing in the same space. But those organizations that prepare themselves ahead of time with a strategy on how to implement and secure the IoT within their environment can avoid some costly and potentially dangerous lessons.

Scenario #1: Attacks intended to cause physical damage. We've already seen several instances where a cyber attack has led to real world damage, and that's with a very limited amount of network connected devices capable of doing such a thing. The IoT would change that, putting a plethora of devices online capable of making physical changes. Something as simple as a pressure gauge, a security door, a furnace, or an HVAC unit, given enough internet connected functionality, could be hacked and changed to a point that it caused material damage.

Scenario #2: Data breach through a seemingly harmless device. As part of the interconnectivity mentioned earlier, any IoT device that has access to other devices, or to a central computer, can be used as an entry point for further access. It's unlikely you'd have your toaster set up to SSH [Secure Shell, a network protocol for operating services securely over an unsecured network] into your home security system, but it's more likely that a business would install a myriad of devices and, either through negligence or lack of ability, fail to secure each and every one. Compliance standards will help to regulate the methods by which organizations can protect themselves from these attacks.

Scenario #3: Unauthorized access to services. Finally, without interrupting or damaging anything, malicious actors could simply collect the data generated by these devices and use or sell it however they see fit. Access restriction to the services and information IoT devices provide must be enforced to prevent unauthorized data mining.

The truth is we as a society, as a species, are still struggling to live in a world where the technology we've created has accelerated everything we do. We live in a time of great possibility, for good and bad, but often without the requisite time to stop and think.

Compliance standards are mostly reactive, with some foresight given to emerging trends, but focused mostly on known threats and problems. There will be a time when IoT devices become integrated into business practices, but before the compliance standards are written to secure them; some cutting edge organizations already face this issue. The admittedly large upside of IoT devices may coax some businesses into deploying them without fully considering the consequences, just as the initial digitization of business, still in process, came with little security.

What can be done then? As technology cycles out, the less time an organization has to spend reinventing the wheel of how it does business, the more it can focus on the business itself. Here are some key steps businesses can take to prepare for the IoT, especially if they fall under compliance standards that require documentation for audits.

- Functionality is not enough. Remember that making it work is only part of what's required when establishing devices with network connectivity. Security should be factored in from the earliest planning stages, taking just as prominent a role as functionality. For cost saving reasons, this is often not the case, but in the long term, a solid information security policy and perspective will save money, time and possible reputation.
- Visibility. As devices proliferate, it's important to have a good system to track inventory, configuration, changes, etc. Even the complexity of a modern data center requires this kind of visibility to smoothly operate, so something as potentially intricate as the IoT will require organizations to have unparalleled visibility into their environments. The reason companies get breached is that someone outside the company sees a flaw or, more likely, a misconfiguration, before someone from the IT team sees and fixes it. By improving visibility, organizations can stay on top of what's actually happening.
- Testing. Full visibility can only be obtained through regular testing to ensure expected configurations behave the way they are supposed to. By comparing the existing state of an environment to a desired state as defined by the organization, IT teams can know immediately when an asset falls out of compliance or a configuration is changed.
- Insurance. Security is like trying to go the speed of light: at best you can only get 99.9% there, and "at best" is rarely the scenario for cyber security. But whether you have a .1% gap or a 10% gap, you need to cover the remainder with a policy to protect your business in the event of a breach or major outage. Risk, and the resulting cost of coverage, depend on the particular security configuration, and environments

with more security would be less likely to need their policies over time.

- Agility. Traditional IT shops have often been resistant to change. Change is what breaks things. This approach leads to a rusted in place infrastructure, fragile systems no one wants to touch and siloed knowledge. In an environment like this, implementing new technology, much less new compliance standards for that technology, causes dread and sometimes feet dragging, preventing projects from completing in a timely manner. But with the visibility and testing mechanisms mentioned above, change doesn't have to be such a nightmare.

It can be difficult enough for a business to keep up with its particular IT environment, much less the IT field at large, but although it may seem counterintuitive, factoring in the way technology changes, its lifecycles, into everyday IT procedures makes the management of the particular environment much easier. Just like software development and deployment has been revolutionized by automation and DevOps (or DevOps-like) ideas, the way a business maintains its technological infrastructure should reflect the realities, good and bad, of an expanding and accelerating digital footprint, rather than continually trying to shove the square peg of their environment into a space that's constantly changing shape.

Organizations to Contact

The editors have compiled the following list of organizations concerned with the issues debated in this book. The descriptions are derived from materials provided by the organizations. All have publications or information available for interested readers. This list was compiled on the date of publication of the present volume; the information provided here may change. Be aware that many organizations take several weeks or longer to respond to inquiries, so allow as much time as possible.

The CDAC Internet of Things (IoT) Lab

Center for Data and Computing
John Crerar Library Building
5730 South Ellis Avenue
Suite 263
Chicago, IL 60637
(773) 834-2985
email: cdac@uchicago.edu
website: www.cdac.uchicago.edu/iot-lab

This lab run by the University of Chicago's Center for Data and Computing directs much of the school's experimental work with the latest applications of the internet of things. Researchers at the lab do everything from replicating home broadband networks in order to determine how accessible new IoT applications might be to applying data science and IoT-powered machine learning techniques to uncover new insights in other fields. At its heart, the University of Chicago's lab is at the forefront of finding new possibilities for the IoT that go beyond consumer-level applications.

Cloud Security Alliance

2212 Queen Anne Avenue
N. Seattle, WA 98109
(656) 475-1724
email: support@cloudsecurityalliance.org
website: www.cloudsecurityalliance.org

A Seattle-based collection of businesses and governments, the Cloud Security Alliance operates a popular cloud security provider certification program called the CSA Security, Trust & Assurance Registry. The group also employs a network of security professionals that offer security work for users. Elsewhere, the group often plays host to changing federal internet regulation: in 2011, the Obama administration announced its cloud computing strategy at the organization's annual summit.

IERC-European Research Cluster on the Internet of Things

email: Ovidiu.Vermesan@sintef.no
website: www.internet-of-things-research.eu/about_ierc.htm

A European research group that works toward developing and defining a common vision of how IoT technology should be used, this group largely focuses on directing projects throughout the European Union. Some of the projects that it's associated with include efforts to bridge the IoT's interoperability gap and promote new ways of enabling IoT-operability in mass-market products. The group has also hosted multiple conferences around the world since 2010.

Industrial Internet Consortium

9C Medway Road, PMB 274
Milford, MA 01757
(781) 444-0404
email: info@iiconsortium.org
website: www.iiconsortium.org

The Industrial Internet Consortium is a group of 258 different companies but was initially founded by just five: AT&T, Cisco, General Electric, IBM, and Intel. The five are giants of the tech sector and their group lobbies politically on behalf of how those companies use the internet of things. Elsewhere, the group also operates a number of testbeds that experiment and help market newer applications of the IoT.

Institute for the Wireless Internet of Things

Northeastern University
716 Columbus Avenue, 190 CP
Boston, MA 02120
(617) 373-4897
email: wiot@northeastern.edu
website: www.northeastern.edu/wiot

Launched by Northeastern University in 2019, the Institute for the Wireless Internet of Things was started with funding from the school, as well as $25 million from the federal government via the National Science Foundation, the Department of Homeland Security, and the Department of Defense, among other agencies. But the institute is only the federal government's latest IoT-related investment in the university: some of those agencies started running a massive data center at the school called Colosseum, which calls itself the world's most powerful emulator of wireless networks. One of the school's more recent projects, which is currently being run through the institute, is called Platforms for Advanced Wireless Research, which researches ways to power the IoT on a city-wide scale.

Integrated Innovation Institute

4612 Forbes Avenue
Pittsburgh, PA 15213
(844) 629-0200
email: iii@cmu.edu

website: www.cmu.edu A joint initiative of Carnegie Mellon University's College of Engineering, its College of Fine Arts, and its Tepper School of Business, the III conducts extensive research and experimentation involving new uses of the internet of things. Some of the initiative's recent projects include research into agricultural uses of IoT-powered irrigation and developing IoT devices that better assist the visually impaired, and, in one case, students at the school designed an IoT device that helps couples communicate emotionally.

Internet of Business
501 Boylston Street
Boston, MA 02116
(781) 247-1830
email: info@internetofbusiness.com
website: www.internetofbusiness.com

Based in the college mecca of Boston, the Internet of Business was created to help businesses "leverage the technology advancing job roles," according to its website. The group is always sourcing new case studies on how the internet of things is being used and is a great resource to find some of the latest white papers being published on the subject. The group's website regularly publishes shorter and more accessible editorial posts as well.

The Internet of Things Consortium
(310) 266-2477
email: Membership@iofthings.org
website: www.iofthings.org

This business development group focused on, of all things, the internet of things. The group is behind industry events like the IoTC NEXT: The Connected Future Summit, which had its first run in 2019. The group focuses on what it calls the core areas of IoT technology today: smart cities, home automation, wearables, connected cars, and retail transformation.

The Internet Society

11710 Plaza America Drive
Suite 400
Reston, VA 20190
(703) 439-2120
email: isoc@isoc.org
website: www.isoc.org

The Internet Society is a business group that focuses on developing new standards, protocols, and the technical infrastructure of the internet. Among its projects, the most well-known is the Internet Engineering Task Force, which gathers together network designers, operators, vendors, and researchers to develop open standards for the changing varieties of internet use. "Open standards are a cornerstone of the Internet," the group says on its website.

IoT ONE

338 Nanjing West Road
Tian'an Center, Shanghai
China
email: team@iotone.com
website: www.iotone.com

A consulting firm with offices in Shanghai, Cologne, Singapore, and Lausanne, IoT ONE is just one of the many businesses that help clients mitigate the threats and adapt to take advantage of the opportunities that the internet of things presents businesses around the world. But in addition to its consulting work, IoT ONE also hosts thousands of case studies on how the internet of things is being used around the world. Some of the companies that IoT ONE has worked with include GE, Siemens, and Bayer.

IoT Research Center
107 S Indiana Avenue
Bloomington, IN 47405
(812) 855-4848
email: ljcamp@indiana.edu
website: www.iot.luddy.indiana.edu

A project run by Indiana University–Bloomington, the IoT Research Center focuses on "addressing human aspects and technical aspects" of the internet of things. Led by three professors at the public university, as well as a colleague from the University of Washington, the center works on projects like developing cybersecurity educational tools and combatting system vulnerabilities. Beyond the human and the technical aspects of the internet of things, the center also studies the broader impact of how the IoT will likely change society as a whole.

IoT Systems Research Center
1513 University Avenue
Madison WI, 53706
(608) 265-9872
email: iotcenter@engr.wisc.edu
website: www.iotcenter.engr.wisc.edu

Operated by the University of Wisconsin–Madison College of Engineering, the IoT Systems Research Center is a partnership between the publicly funded school and companies like BP, A. O. Smith, and IBM. These resources allow the center to process industrial data analytics as well as study topics like industrial process simulation, productivity analysis, scheduling, and planning. The center also regularly hosts conferences on the subject.

Bibliography

Books

Erik Brynjolfsson. *The Second Machine Age: Work, Progress, and Prosperity in a Time of Brilliant Technologies.* New York, NY: W. W. Norton & Company, 2014.

Nicholas Carr. *The Shallows: What the Internet Is Doing to Our Brains.* New York, NY: W. W. Norton & Company, 2011.

Sunil Cheruvu, Anil Kumar, Ned Smith, and David M. Wheeler. *Demystifying Internet of Things Security: Successful IoT Device/Edge and Platform Security Deployment.* New York, NY: Apress, 2019.

Laura DeNardis. *The Internet in Everything: Freedom and Security in a World with No Off Switch.* New Haven, CT: Yale University Press, 2020.

Carolina Fortuna and John Davies (ed.). *The Internet of Things: From Data to Insight.* Hoboken, NJ: Wiley, 2020.

Adam Greenfield. *The Dawning Age of Ubiquitous Computing.* San Francisco, CA: Peachpit, 2006.

Adam Greenfield. *Radical Technologies: The Design of Everyday Life.* Brooklyn, NY: Verso, 2017.

Samuel Greengard. *The Internet of Things.* Cambridge, MA: MIT Press, 2015.

Daniel Kellmereit and Daniel Obodovski. *The Silent Intelligence: The Internet of Things.* Grove City, MN: DND Ventures, 2013.

Maciej Kranz. *Building the Internet of Things: Implement New Business Models, Disrupt Competitors, Transform Your Industry.* Hoboken, NJ: Wiley, 2016.

Peter Lucas. *Trillions: Thriving in the Emerging Information Ecology.* Hoboken, NJ: Wiley, 2012.

Gretchen McCulloch. *Because Internet: Understanding the New Rules of Language.* New York, NY: Penguin Random House, 2019.

Adrian McEwen and Hakim Cassimally. *Designing the Internet of Things.* Hoboken, NJ: Wiley, 2013.

Bruce Schneier. *Click Here to Kill Everybody.* New York, NY: W. W. Norton & Company, 2018.

Klaus Schwab. *The Fourth Industrial Revolution.* New York, NY: Penguin Random House, 2016.

Bruce Sinclair. *IoT Inc: How Your Company Can Use the Internet of Things to Win in the Outcome Economy.* New York, NY: McGraw-Hill Education, 2017.

Peter Waher. *Learning Internet of Things.* Birmingham, UK: Packt, 2015.

Periodicals and Internet Sources

Tyler Cowen, "When Products Talk," *New Yorker*, June 1, 2016. www.newyorker.com/business/currency/when-products -talk

Adam Davidson, "A Washing Machine That Tells the Future," *New Yorker*, October 23, 2017. www.newyorker.com /magazine/2017/10/23/a-washing-machine-that-tells-the -future

The Economist, "How the World Will Change as Computers Spread into Everyday Objects," September 12, 2019. www .economist.com/leaders/2019/09/12/how-the-world-will -change-as-computers-spread-into-everyday-objects

The Economist, "The Internet of Things Will Bring the Internet's Business Model into the Rest of the World," September 12, 2019. www.economist.com/technology

-quarterly/2019/09/12/the-internet-of-things-will-bring
-the-internets-business-model-into-the-rest-of-the-world

Sue Halpern, "The Terrifying Potential of the 5G Network," *New Yorker*, April 26, 2019. www.newyorker.com/news /annals-of-communications/the-terrifying-potential-of-the -5g-network

Farhad Manjoo, "A Future Where Everything Becomes a Computer Is as Creepy as You Feared," *New York Times*, October 10, 2018. www.nytimes.com/2018/10/10 /technology/future-internet-of-things.html

William Neuman and Luis Jaime Castillo Butters, "The Internet of Things Is Coming for Us," *New York Times*, January 21, 2017. www.nytimes.com/2017/01/21/sunday-review /the-internet-of-things-is-coming-for-us.html

Lily Hay Newman, "Why Ring Doorbells Perfectly Exemplify the IoT Security Crisis," *Wired*, December 12, 2019. www .wired.com/story/ring-hacks-exemplify-iot-security-crisis

Jennifer Strong, "'Internet of Battlefield Things' Transforms Combat," *Wall Street Journal*, October 24, 2018. blogs .wsj.com/cio/2018/10/24/internet-of-battlefield-things -transforms-combat

Irving Wladawsky-Berger, "The Internet of Things Is Changing the World," *Wall Street Journal*, January 10, 2020. blogs.wsj .com/cio/2020/01/10/the-internet-of-things-is-changing -the-world

Jonathan Zittrain, "From Westworld to Best World for the Internet of Things," *New York Times*, June 3, 2018. www .nytimes.com/2018/06/03/opinion/westworld-internet-of -things.html

Index

A

agriculture, applications of
  IoT in, 91–94, 141–142
agriculture drones, 92
Apple, 24, 119, 128
Ashton, Kevin, 104
Atkinson, Robert, 38

B

Baysal, Nur, 144–148
Beren, David, 23–25
blockchain technology, 128–
  131, 144–148
Bridle, James, 118

C

Castillo, Andrea, 39–42
Clark, David, 38
clothing, networked, 39–42
commercial IoT, 49–52

D

dark fiber, 68–74
data, ownership of, 29, 83, 102
Davies, John, 30, 31
DeNardis, Laura, 33–35
Donath, Judith, 37
Dowling, Michael, 145

F

Fairfield, Joshua A. T., 64–67
food systems, sustainability of,
  95–103

G

geoconquesting, 51
geofencing, 50–51
Google, 19, 22, 24, 39, 62, 67,
  119, 128

H

Harris, John, 117–120
health care, and the IoT,
  21–22, 40, 41, 53, 56–57,
  133, 140
Hearst, Marti, 37
Higgins, Stuart, 31
Holden, Nicholas M., 95–103

I

industrial internet of things
  (IIoT), 44–48
internet of food, 95–103
internet of things (IoT)
  and children's toys, 153–156
  in the commercial world,
    49–52

and communities of color, 53–59

and environmental degradation, 76–79

environmental impact of, 104–116

explanations of, 19–20, 40, 104, 132

and people with disabilities, 23–25, 133

and safety/security, 16, 20–21, 33–35, 46–47, 65, 128–131, 137, 149–152, 153–156

K

Kobie, Nicole, 19–22
Kshetri, Nir, 128–131
Kumar, Sachin, 132–143

L

Lange, Matthew C., 95–103
Lee, Nicol Turner, 53–60
livestock monitoring, 92–93

M

manufacturing, and the IoT, 21, 31, 44, 45, 46, 47, 108, 114, 143
Maras, Marie-Helen, 153–156
Matthews, Kayla, 49–52, 61–63
McCarthy, Lauren, 68–74
McClelland, Calum, 44–48

McCloskey, Deirdre, 148
McFadin, Patrick, 122–127
McGlynn, Brian, 26–29
Microsoft, 23, 128, 129, 145
Muraleedharan, Sarath, 76–79

O

Oldfield, Thomas L., 95–103
Oluwafemi, Temitope, 149–152

P

phishing attacks, 35
precision farming, 91–92
predictive maintenance, 45
Project Jacquard, 39, 41–42

R

Radu, Laura-Diana, 104–116
Ravindra, Savaram, 90–94
recycling, and the IoT, 86–87, 88, 109

S

Samsung, 67, 128
Schneier, Bruce, 15
Sequeira, Neil, 86–89
Silva, Christianna, 36–38
smart cities, 20, 30, 31, 32, 34, 68–74, 80–84, 87, 105, 115, 141, 142
smart clothes, 39–42
smart farming, 90–94
smart homes, 20, 24, 46, 66, 77, 83, 114, 141, 153

Stanislawski, Stefan, 31–32
Sundararajan, Aruna, 63

T

Thierer, Adam, 40, 146, 147
Thilthorpe, Adam, 30
Tiwari, Prayag, 132–143
transportation industry, and
    the IoT, 26–29, 141

U

UpGuard, 157–163

W

waste management, and the
    IoT, 78, 86–89
Webb, Amy, 38
White, Eoin P., 95–103
Wright, Tim, 30–32

Z

Zhang, Shufan, 80–85
Zymbler, Mikhail, 132–143